NEW ROUTES
TO LIBRARY SUCCESS

ALA Editions purchases fund advocacy,

awareness, and accreditation programs

for library professionals worldwide.

NEW ROUTES
TO LIBRARY SUCCESS

100+ IDEAS
from Outside the Stacks

Elisabeth Doucett

ala
editions

AN IMPRINT OF THE AMERICAN LIBRARY ASSOCIATION
CHICAGO | 2015

ELISABETH DOUCETT is the director of Curtis Memorial Library in Brunswick, Maine. In addition to a master's degree from the Simmons College Graduate School of Library and Information Science, Ms. Doucett has an MBA in marketing from the Kellogg Graduate School of Management at Northwestern University. She is author of the books *Creating Your Library Brand* and *What They Don't Teach You at Library School*, both published by the American Library Association. Ms. Doucett speaks and teaches nationally, generally focusing on the topics of library marketing, branding, and trend tracking.

© 2015 by the American Library Association

Extensive effort has gone into ensuring the reliability of the information in this book; however, the publisher makes no warranty, express or implied, with respect to the material contained herein.

ISBNs
978-0-8389-1313-0 (paper)
978-0-8389-1319-2 (PDF)
978-0-8389-1320-8 (ePub)
978-0-8389-1321-5 (Kindle)

Library of Congress Cataloging-in-Publication Data
Doucett, Elisabeth.
  New routes to library success : 100+ ideas from outside the stacks / Elisabeth Doucett.
     pages cm
  Includes bibliographical references and index.
  ISBN 978-0-8389-1313-0 (paper)
  1. Public libraries–Administration. 2. Public services (Libraries) 3. Libraries–Customer services. 4. Libraries and community. 5. Curtis Memorial Library (Brunswick, Me.) 6. Entrepreneurship–Case studies. 7. Creative ability in business–Case studies. 8. Businesspeople–Interviews. 9. Organizational change. 10. Organizational effectiveness. I. Title.
  Z678.D58 2015
  025.1'974–dc23

                               2014046369

Cover design by Alejandra Diaz. Imagery © Shutterstock, Inc.
Text design and composition by Pauline Neuwirth in the ITC New Baskerville Std and Brandon Grotesque typefaces.

♾ This paper meets the requirements of ANSI/NISO Z39.48-1992
(Permanence of Paper).

Printed in the United States of America

19 18 17 16 15   5 4 3 2 1

To my husband and my mother

CONTENTS

PREFACE

• WHY THIS BOOK •

I worry about the future of libraries. I have been a library professional only since 2004, and even in 2004 most of the people who planned to work in a library understood that things were changing. It was clear that libraries were in a period of rapid transition and evolution, driven by the explosion of technology that was everywhere. Those of us who graduated from library school at that time all knew that we had to find new ways for libraries to operate and serve their communities or libraries would slowly start dying off as they became irrelevant. Ever since I started working in this profession, I have fretted about whether we library professionals are moving fast enough and being creative enough to move our institutions into the right place for the future.

As the result of being a worrywart and wanting to make sure that the library at which I am the director (Curtis Memorial Library in Brunswick, Maine) successfully makes the transition to a technology-driven, digitally dominated future, I spend a great deal of time identifying and evaluating new library programs, processes, and management methods. In the past few years, I have struggled to find new ideas that went beyond being programmatic to being strategic and broad based enough to drive substantial change. There have been some wonderful, intriguing programs being developed, such as public library support of the makerspace movement. However, I have always thought that new programs are not enough to get to the heart of the challenge that libraries face: their very real need to redefine their entire role in their communities. To get to that level of transformative change, libraries must discover what their communities need and want in today's world, redefining their mission accordingly, and then adjust their operations to support that mission.

I decided that I needed to cast a much wider net if I was going to find new ideas for Curtis Library that would have a substantial impact on the library. But, how do you find and develop ideas that can make a real, substantive difference? I decided that the first place to look was not other libraries but other professions. As library professionals I think we miss out on opportunities because we do not often enough tap the ideas, innovations, and ways of working of different professions. When I started as a librarian, I regularly looked to business (which was my first career) for ideas that could transfer from one environment to the other. Businesses spend huge sums of money and employ highly intelligent people to run them. Libraries can benefit from their expertise simply by seeking out friendly people in the business world who are willing to share ideas and help libraries in the process. So, based on my past experience and my desire to identify innovative opportunities, I determined that I would primarily focus on talking to businesspeople to see if I could find some great ideas for my library. If I found other good contacts along the way, I would certainly incorporate them into the mix.

My hope in talking to people in the business community was also that I would discover not just *new* ideas but also *transformative* ideas— ideas that will help libraries take a giant leap forward into the future. Incremental change is slightly improving something that already exists. Transformative change is something that has a major impact and will drive an organization forward in large leaps versus small increments. The need for transformative change was solidified and defined for me when I read *The Business Model Innovation Factory: How to Stay Relevant When the World Is Changing* (what a perfect subtitle for capturing the attention of a librarian) by Saul Kaplan (Wiley, 2012) after attending a talk by him at Bowdoin College, also located in Brunswick, Maine. One of Kaplan's theories is that ideas for transformative change can best be found in the "gray space" between professions, meaning neither my world nor yours but a place where we both can learn from each other. Kaplan calls this principle "Enable Random Collisions of Unusual Suspects," which says it all. If we step outside our normal milieu and enter that gray space and talk to people who do not inhabit our world, he posits that it becomes more likely that we will find ideas with the power and energy to transform our own world. In contrast, if we stay in our normal rut (oops—routine!), the likelihood is high that our ideas for change will be incremental versus transformative.

Incremental change is taking what we have always done and doing it a bit better, and this is not a bad thing. However, professions that are being challenged to rationalize their very existence (like librarianship) need to search for the big ideas that will move the profession into its next evolution. Kaplan's theory is that you can never bust out of your old way of existing if you are not willing to pursue transformative change. Pursuing new ideas for libraries by talking to smart people and in the process seeking ideas that will help drive transformative change then became the goals for this book. My thanks go to Saul Kaplan and his book *The Business Model Innovation Factory* for articulating the ideas that had been swirling around in my head and helping me figure out what I wanted to discover as I started doing this research.

• HOW TO READ THIS BOOK •

The first chapter in this book defines the process that I developed and used to interview people in the business environment. The process is simple and is meant to make it easy for you, the reader, to go out and explore your own gray spaces. I suggest that you begin reading with chapter 1, even though it is process oriented, because it will give you a good starting point for defining your own methodology to enable you to do your own research.

Each chapter thereafter is based on an interview with an individual who worked in a business or organization that I thought might be able to provide new ideas for libraries. My goal in each interview was to identify learning that could be translated into implications for libraries. After defining the implications for libraries from the learning, I brainstormed to develop specific ideas about how libraries might turn those implications into actions. My goal in sharing these ideas is not to imply that these are the best or only ideas but simply to show that any library could use what I learned to develop concrete next steps for implementation. Please feel free to use these ideas as a starting point for developing your own ideas.

At the beginning of each chapter, I briefly articulate why I chose that particular organization and individual(s) to interview and what I hoped to learn. Sometimes I learned exactly what I had planned on learning and I collected a great deal of information. Sometimes the learning had absolutely nothing to do with my original expectations. In either case, I share here what I discovered. The most important thing I found in this process was being flexible and open to wherever the interviews led because I invariably learned something useful. I include a summary of what I learned at the end of each chapter and identify the learning that seemed to have the potential to be transformative for libraries. Some of what I learned was not new or transformative in my mind, but I include everything under the assumption that it might be useful to another library.

I wrote one chapter, "Content Curation," without the benefit of interviews. I sought out input from several companies that are known to be experts at content curation but was not able to get interviews. I decided that I would write the chapter anyway because my fifteen years of business background gives me enough of a knowledge base to interpret the concept of content curation and make it available to libraries as a potential tool. I think it provides a potentially powerful opportunity for libraries, so I very much wanted to include it in this book.

This book is about what you can learn from *talking* to people outside the library profession. So, in writing it, I did not do a great deal of additional research. However, if an interviewee recommended a book or had written a book that spoke to the topic at hand, I did read it. Also, if I found a good online resource about a specific topic, I read that. At the end of each chapter, I identify these resources in case you are inclined to do more reading.

I also include at the end of each chapter the list of questions that I put together for each interview. I developed the questions to learn more about what I saw as each company's expertise. I discovered during some interviews that I was able to get every single question answered, but, more often, I was lucky to get half of the questions asked since the conversations frequently went off on tangents as they progressed. I was perfectly happy to pursue the train of thought of the interviewee, and I found that a lot of rich information came up by letting the conversation flow. If you decide to use the process in this book, please feel free to use any of the questions I have developed. I recommend, however, that you also pursue a policy of letting the interviewees direct the conversation if they are so inclined. You may not even know the best question to ask until you hear the answer from an interviewee. Experts in different fields have such a wealth of experience and knowledge that you can learn a great deal from them, even if they never answer a single one of your questions.

My goal in writing is to provide information that will be easy to understand and practical so that this book can serve as a how-to manual for those who would like to try the same type of research. I would like to hear comments from fellow librarians about whether I have achieved any of my goals in terms of making my writing realistic and immediately useful. If you would like to follow up with me about anything I have written, please feel free to leave comments at my blog: www.irreverentlibrarian.com. Thank you for reading this book.

ACKNOWLEDGMENTS

My special thanks go to the individuals who spent their personal time and energy to share their thinking with me: Josh Davis (Gelato Fiasco), Margot Atwell (Kickstarter), Walter Briggs (Briggs Advertising), Fritz Grobe (EepyBird), Chris Wilson (L.L.Bean), Vicki Loomis (Trendwatching.com), Kate Cheney Chappell (Tom's of Maine), Meredith Jones (Maine Community Foundation), and Brian Kevin and Ginny Wright (*Down East* magazine). All of these individuals were very supportive and helpful and willing to explore the idea that they might know something that would be helpful to libraries. I cannot thank them enough for their help.

I would also like to thank the Board of Directors at Curtis Memorial Library. They are a far-sighted, smart group of people who care tremendously about the library as a community resource. They do whatever it takes to help the library and its staff, including providing me with the time and unqualified support to write this book, for which I would like to offer a heartfelt thank-you. To paraphrase Meredith Jones from the Maine Community Foundation, "I am lucky to be able to do such joyous work!"

1

THE PROCESS

• BACKGROUND •

Breaking out of your day-to-day routine and doing something totally outside your comfort zone can be difficult. I found developing a process for writing this book and then executing that process was often nerve-wracking because it meant I was talking to people who were not librarians, who did not always understand what I did for a living, and who were very busy. I had to explain what I was trying to do (quickly!) and convince them that there was value in participating. Sometimes I was better at this than at other times, and sometimes I got "No!" for an answer almost before I had asked the question. On the positive side, I had fascinating conversations with the people I interviewed and I walked away feeling energized and full of new ideas. I also reaffirmed my perspective that basically the world is filled with interesting people who are more than willing to help a stranger. Based on my experience, I think that those in charge of running a library can benefit hugely from talking to people outside their normal sphere of activity. Such interactions can open your eyes to new ways of working, and they have the added benefit of being tremendously invigorating.

I had two goals for this book. The first was to identify ideas that had the power to drive transformative change for libraries. I planned to do this by talking to organizations, identifying what they did well, clarifying the implications of how they operated for libraries, and defining new ideas that might help libraries in their effort to evolve and develop new ways of serving their communities. I planned to interview businesspeople primarily, but I also talked with a representative of one nonprofit organization with an outstanding reputation as a great workplace because I was sure the interview would provide helpful input.

My second goal in writing this book was to develop a process that library professionals could use to do their own interviews since my areas of focus and interest might not be right for a library community different from my own (Curtis Memorial Library serves a population of approximately 25,000, including the college town of Brunswick, Maine, which is home to Bowdoin College). By developing a procedure that is easy to follow, I hope to encourage library professionals to try this research on their own so that they can find the perfect transformative ideas for their own libraries.

• KEY STEPS IN THE PROCESS •

STEP ONE: *Identify what you want to learn from talking to an organization.* My particular areas of interest were those ways of thinking and operating that I thought could help move libraries in new strategic or operational directions in the future:

- Creativity in how a library thinks and operates
- Customer service that is top quality and intrinsic to how the library staff interact with the public
- How to build a library culture that is comfortable doing things differently from accepted norms
- What an entrepreneurial organization does to make it nimble and responsive so it can accomplish all of the above
- How to create an outstanding workplace that acts as a magnet for the best employees

- How to "learn your community"—the people, the events, the direction it is headed—to ensure that your library is providing the right services
- How to research and use trends to make your library more responsive to your community
- How libraries can support the "creators" (artists, musicians, writers) in their communities
- How to use content curation to attract new users to the library
- How unconventional thinkers work and what makes them successful

Please note that these were areas in which I was interested. You might have a completely different list of processes or concepts that you would like to explore for your library, and you can easily do that.

STEP TWO: *Identify organizations that match your learning needs and schedule interviews.* I identified companies both locally and nationally that I thought did a great job at one of the areas of opportunity identified above. I then started approaching companies to find contacts. My goal was to get the name of a person at each company and make contact with that individual by e-mail first and then by telephone to see if he or she would be willing to participate in an interview. I planned originally to have a combination of national, regional, and local companies.

Early on in the process, I discovered that it was tough to get an interview with the national companies unless you had a direct contact, but it was surprisingly easy to get interviews at the regional and local levels. If you decide to follow this process, I suggest approaching the businesses in your town and state first to see if you can schedule interviews. If you decide that there are national companies you must interview but you do not have any contacts, start by talking to their media relations departments (which most large companies have). Generally, the people who work in these departments are very helpful, and if it is possible, they will try to set you up with a good contact. Do not be discouraged. I would estimate that this works about half the time, but the companies that do respond seem to be well worth the effort.

Finally, as you call and send out e-mails to get interviews, make sure that you can explain to each interviewee what the benefit is for him or her in spending valuable time doing an interview with you. I usually said that the interviewee would be helping libraries by doing an interview—and who does not want to help libraries? I would then add that the positive PR (public relations) from doing this for libraries could only be beneficial for the business. Couching it in these terms more often than not meant that I ended up talking with people who were library supporters in their own communities and were happy to help in any way they could.

STEP THREE: *Research each interviewee's company.* Always make sure that you know as much as you reasonably can about the company behind the interviewee. This will help you develop the list of questions discussed in step four. It also demonstrates that you are truly interested in the work that you are doing since you put time and effort into research. That, in turn, will make the interviewee more comfortable and (hopefully) more willing to share information with you. Company websites are a good place to start. I also usually did an article search to discover if there was any "new news" about the company of which I should be aware.

STEP FOUR: *Develop a list of questions for each interview.* I developed a new list of questions for each interview because I was trying to learn something different each time I talked to someone. Because I wanted to make sure that the answers to these questions would be relevant to libraries, I went through each list multiple times asking myself, "If I get an answer to this question, will it identify an idea or piece of information that can help libraries?" I have included the questions I developed for each interview at the end of each chapter. Feel free to use these lists as a starting point for developing your own interview questions.

STEP FIVE: *Confirm each appointment the day before.* This may seem obvious, but I did not do this for my first three interviews and something went wrong with each one. Either I got the time of the appointment wrong, or the person I was interviewing did, or the place for the interview was wrong—you get the idea. Confirm everything the day before and do it in writing. You will be glad you did.

STEP SIX: *Confirm with your interviewee how much time he or she has available.* Stick to this time limit even if you have more that you would like to discuss. Your interviewees will appreciate your being respectful of their time and you will end by having made a good contact for the future. You can always e-mail additional questions after the interview. Generally, most people are comfortable with answering post-interview questions as long as you do not overdo it.

STEP SEVEN: *Allow the interview to go where it will, but do not let it go so far afield that you cannot use the information being provided.* You have a list of questions and hopefully you will get at least some of them answered. However, if the interview goes off down a path that you did not expect but you see potential in where it is going, let it go. Sometimes the best information comes from places you never anticipated. Also, do not be surprised if you go to talk about a specific topic like customer service and the interview ends up being focused on something different like creativity. Again, if there is value, let it flow.

The only caveat to this is that you should work very hard during the interview to keep your own opinions to yourself and not to interject too much of your own perspective. Because I was so interested in what my interviewees had to say, sometimes I would respond to their comments with one of my own and what was supposed to be an interview turned into more of a conversation. A good discussion is never a bad thing, but the goal for your interviews is to learn from others, not to offer your own opinions, unless that will help the interview process.

STEP EIGHT: *Tape your discussion.* Even if you are not going to write a book when you are done, taping the interview is very helpful. It allows you to go back and check what you think you heard. I used the app AudioNote that both records and allows you to take notes as you are interviewing. It also lets you go back and add notes if you listen to an interview a second or third time.

STEP NINE: *Do not forget to say thank you.* Again, this one seems simple and obvious, but it is so important to remember. People are taking the time to share their thoughts and creativity with you. I cannot imagine a more valuable gift, and I want to make sure those people know that I appreciate it. Depending on the person and organization, I sent either a handwritten thank-you or an e-mail. If you can, I recommend keeping in touch with your interviewees. They can be a wonderful resource for your library in the future. If you end up doing a presentation or writing an article about what you learned, make sure you share a copy with each person interviewed. They will appreciate hearing what you discovered and it will help maintain the relationship.

STEP TEN: *Write down what you think are the implications of your interview, but do not immediately start developing ideas for your library.* I am a big believer in letting ideas "percolate" and making your subconscious mind do some of the heavy lifting. Generally, I would sit down a day or two after an interview to review the audio and to make any notes that I missed during the interview. I would also identify the big implications that I could see right away. Then, I would put everything away for a week or so and let my mind work on it. When I finally sat down to start writing, I was always amazed at how quickly the ideas for my library started to become clear.

STEP ELEVEN: *Brainstorm ideas based on what you have learned.* I suggest that you do this both by yourself and with a group of supportive colleagues. Brainstorming alone can be a very productive enterprise, but if you include colleagues, they may go down paths that you have not even considered. Put together a list of every idea that comes up. Do not throw out any ideas, because what is not appropriate today might be tomorrow's breakthrough concept. Put the list away for a day or two and then go back to it to see if you have any additional ideas to add.

STEP TWELVE: *Narrow the focus of the ideas you want to execute and get buy-in and support from your governing body.* Prioritize your ideas into two categories. Some of the ideas that you brainstorm may be obvious and executed quickly, so you can get moving on them right away. However, some of the ideas may truly be transformational in nature. If you are going to make substantial changes in how you do business, it makes sense to get understanding and buy-in from your governing group before you start moving. My suggestion is to develop a one-page proposal for each idea that includes a complete definition of the idea, the resources that would be required to execute the idea (people, money, equipment), the potential risks and rewards of pursuing this idea, and a timetable for execution. A proposal makes it very easy to present ideas to your library's leadership, and it makes it easy for them to determine whether they are interested in pursuing those ideas.

Finally, keep in mind the nature of entrepreneurship (see chapter 2). Entrepreneurs test, test, and test ideas because if something is not going to work, they want to know that as soon as possible so that they can quickly move on to the next idea. You should do the same. Do not spend too much time researching an idea or too much money testing an idea. Get ideas out into your library quickly and inexpensively. See how they do. If one fails, do not mourn the idea for months—move on to the next one. There is a whole world of ideas to explore and time is short!

2

ENTREPRENEURSHIP

JOSH DAVIS
Gelato Fiasco

• WHY THIS TOPIC •

Entrepreneurs look at a marketplace, see opportunity, and find ways to realize that opportunity. Generally, they are optimistic and interesting people and the businesses they start are full of energy and creative thinking. When you walk in the door of a small start-up, you can feel the passion that everyone involved is bringing to the enterprise. I want libraries to have this same powerful energy that is apparent the minute a library patron walks in the door.

My goal in this interview was to understand at least some of what makes an organization entrepreneurial in nature and to define how a library might adopt those work processes to become faster moving, more responsive, and nimble. Libraries can be very slow in changing and responding to their environments. If they can learn how to be more alert to evolving needs and expectations in their communities and faster in how they react to them, libraries will have learned important skills for surviving and prospering in the future.

• WHY THIS ORGANIZATION •

Given my high regard for entrepreneurs and my own desire to have a library with the same high energy as a start-up, I decided to begin the research for this book by talking to Josh Davis, who is the co-founder (with Bruno Tropeano) of Gelato Fiasco in Brunswick, Maine. Josh is in his early thirties, and I got the impression when I talked to him that he had decided to become an entrepreneur when he was born. He is focused, well educated in business, and obviously passionate about making his business succeed.

The company has two stores, one in Brunswick (the original store) and a second one in Portland, Maine. Gelato Fiasco sells high-quality Italian gelato in a coffee shop type of atmosphere. The staff make the product fresh every day and develop new flavors on a regular basis. You can taste as many flavors as you would like before you make your purchase decision (and plenty of kids in town take full advantage of this opportunity!) The staff at the stores are generally in their twenties and thirties, very pleasant, and more than willing to explain anything that you want to know about the gelato. The company recently also started selling gelato wholesale, making it available for purchase in grocery stores.

Gelato Fiasco has received positive press from the day it opened. Most recently, *Country Living* magazine identified the company as one of the "Made-in-the-USA products crafted from sea to shining sea" in its July 2014 issue and *Down East* magazine readers identified it as the best ice cream in Maine in 2013 and 2014. In April 2014, the Small Business Administration named Josh and Bruno as Young Entrepreneurs of the Year for both Maine and New England. This is definitely a company on its way up, and my hope was to learn as much as possible from how it operates. Josh very kindly gave me a whole morning to talk about Gelato Fiasco, how he and Bruno run the company, his philosophy as an entrepreneur, and what he thinks libraries might learn from how Gelato Fiasco operates.

• INSIGHTS FROM THIS INTERVIEW •

LEARNING

Test, test, test—and fail quickly. Josh is an entrepreneur. By nature he is a risk taker. However, he is a very smart risk taker because he wants the rewards from his business to far exceed the risks in establishing it. One of the ways that he balances risks and rewards becomes quickly obvious in our conversation. He is constantly testing new ideas in every aspect of his business. He tries new flavors. He tries new ways to get people to taste his product. He tries new ways of delivering his product to people who want to buy it. He tries new packaging. However, he balances all of this testing by never committing more than he can afford to lose and by determining quickly if a new idea is going to succeed or not. He does not spend months or years trying to make a product or service perfect before he introduces it to the marketplace, nor does he invest more resources in the development of that product or service than he can afford to lose.

An example of what this entrepreneurial perspective looks like can be seen in the story that Josh told me about how Gelato Fiasco started its wholesale business. They sold the concept of a branded gelato to local restaurants using samples and written storyboards (a series of panels with images that tells the story of the product). They did not dedicate substantial money or equipment to the wholesale business until they knew that they had commitments to purchase the product. Only then did they start purchasing the equipment and resources to deliver products wholesale. Josh said that when they got their first wholesale order, they had to put together an assembly line of staff members to load a pallet because they had not yet invested in the heavy equipment that was needed to do this. This is how entrepreneurs operate. They are optimists and seem always to believe that they can deliver what they have promised, but they will not invest their resources until they know they have a winning idea. Entrepreneurs are willing to take on risk, but they work hard to manage and minimize that risk.

▶ Implication

Libraries can accomplish more, faster, if they allow themselves to test more and fail more. This is such a valuable concept for libraries. As a profession, librarians are hard-wired to "get it right," whether it is finding the book that a patron wants or answering a reference question or helping a parent find the perfect picture book to read to his or her child at bedtime. The downside of this is that we are reluctant to execute programs or ideas or new ways of doing things until we are sure those ideas are guaranteed to succeed. As a result, change often comes slowly to libraries. Sometimes it comes so slowly that libraries completely miss opportunities to provide their communities with needed resources and services.

In addition, because public libraries in particular are funded through tax dollars and are scrutinized on a regular basis against detailed measures of use (number of patrons, borrowing levels, traffic count), there is a definite penalty (reduced funding) associated with failing to meet those measures. The statement that "tax dollars are being wasted" can crop up very quickly if people see any decline in usage statistics. This scares organizations that depend on those tax dollars to open their doors and pay their staff. No library wants to have its tax support reduced because the community feels that it is not being careful with funding.

Despite these concerns, I think the entrepreneur's approach to development is a truly transformative idea for libraries. If libraries can create a culture of controlled experimentation (try, fail, learn, try, succeed), then librarians are held back by only the limits of our own creativity. Perfection is no longer our goal (and perfection is a tough goal to achieve), so we do not have to spend huge amounts of time, energy, and resources to achieve it. Our goal now is to identify the right ideas for our communities. We try out ideas regularly, and if they do not work, then we learn from them and move on. Our ability to be responsive and nimble increases because we are not striving to find perfect ideas but instead are striving for perfect execution (the controlled experimentation) and we trust the process will be a productive one.

▶ Ideas

Educate your library's leadership about controlled experimentation and its potential benefits for your library. Ask for their support to test, test, test, and fail quickly. No one will be willing to take a step into the unknown without knowing that this step will be viewed positively and that trying and failing will be supported, not punished. How do you do this? Start by identifying the positives of the try-and-fail strategy: more creativity in the organization; more willingness to try new ideas; greater sensitivity to changes in the community that need to be responded to with changes in the library; learning from failure instead of having negative consequences for failure. Spend time with your library leadership talking about what this might look like and how it might be implemented. Identify the best- and worst-case scenarios to set expectations appropriately. As different opportunities to try this process come up, make sure that your library's leaders understand what is happening and that the process is transparent from beginning to end. This will help them become vested in understanding its value and in being willing to do this more than once.

Set up a mechanism for collecting ideas to be tested and acknowledging those from whom the ideas come. You want everyone in your entire organization constantly scanning their world for ideas and innovations, and you want them to pass on those ideas so your library's decision makers can consider them. Josh set up an e-mail inbox for this purpose. Anyone on his staff who has an idea can send it to this inbox. Josh also regularly sends ideas and pictures to himself. When he has a quiet moment, he will pull out the ideas that have come in and determine which ones he likes enough to pursue to the next step. By collecting ideas in the moment, you are ensuring that nothing is lost. Also, you need to figure out a way to acknowledge those staff members who contribute ideas. This is critical because people want to know that their work is appreciated. It also increases the likelihood that you will get more ideas in the future.

Change the concept of failure to "What did I learn?" Gelato Fiasco developed a clear, simple, computerized form that staff members fill out after any event run by the business, such as a gelato tasting. This form then goes immediately to Josh and/or Bruno so they get a nearly real-time understanding of what did or did not work at that event. The form is data oriented, not blame oriented. The objective of the form is to identify any and all factors that had an impact on the success of the event. Was there bad weather? Was there another event in town at the same time? Were there problems with equipment or the gelato? All of this information is then reviewed and the learning from it applied to the next event.

Public libraries often struggle to do effective program evaluation. Staffing and resources are so constrained that no sooner have we finished one event, then we are busy moving on to the next event because we do not have the time or people available to figure out if the first event was successful and why or why not. Making assessment and evaluation formal parts of job expectations and then providing the technology to implement these processes would do a great deal to help alleviate the constraints imposed by tight resources. Gelato Fiasco purchases cell phones for employees to ensure that they have the right technology to provide information needed by the company. Ensuring that librarians are equipped with up-to-date technology to support timely and simple evaluation would be a practical way to support a real change in organizational culture. Using technology to facilitate the collection of evaluations is also helpful; the simpler the process is, the less work that it is for the employees involved. Libraries never have enough staff to get the work done. Library directors have to think constantly about the trade-off of giving more work to employees who are already stretched for time, so whatever tools may be available to make data collection simple and seamless are worth searching out.

LEARNING

Libraries and businesses can be pursuing the same goals, giving libraries the chance to learn from the businesses. The idea that a public library should become a "third place" in its community has been around since the early 1990s as Ray Oldenburg's book *The Great Good Place* (now in its third edition; Marlowe & Company, 1999) was read and absorbed by the professional library community. In many ways, libraries have always been "great good places," providing a neutral location where people can gather and have social interactions. However, today many public libraries work actively to fill this niche by providing comfortable seating that encourages sitting and watching the world go by, as well as by adding cafés and making food and/or drink available. Library collections are now reassembled into "neighborhoods" of like-topic books to encourage browsing and spending more time in the library space. Libraries put chairs and small tables anywhere that will encourage folks to sit, relax, and chat.

During our interview, Josh told me that he works actively to make Gelato Fiasco a third place in our community. It had never crossed my mind that another organization in town would be actively trying to do the same thing the library was doing. And, he was putting a lot of thought into this. How? Gelato Fiasco is open seven days a week from 11:00 a.m. until 11:00 p.m. These hours were set intentionally to ensure that customers, who might be looking for a place to hang out, would never have to stop and think about what day it was and what hours the store would be open on that day. Josh wanted to guarantee that anyone looking to get out of the house would know that they could always go to Gelato Fiasco without having to stop to figure out whether the store is open. Even more important, customers would never show up at the store planning to spend time there only to find it closed.

When I asked Josh if he ever thought about a library as a third place, his response was both interesting and disheartening. He said that he would *not* consider a library as a third place because it is a quiet place and the atmosphere is not conducive to social interactions. Furthermore, he saw the library as a "9 to 5 thing" and did not think it was open enough hours in the day to be a social location. He was a bit surprised when I told him that most days of the week the library is open until 8:00 p.m. and that libraries are certainly not the quiet places they used to be. However, whether his perceptions were correct or not, they formed his understanding of the library and so they were real to him.

► Implication

Libraries can learn from businesses that are trying to do some of the same things as libraries. The staff at Curtis Memorial Library have spent many hours thinking about how to do a better job of making Curtis

Library friendly and inviting so that people would see the library as a third place and want to spend more time there. However, we never thought about looking around the community to see who else was doing the same thing and what we might learn from them.

I do not look at these other organizations as "competition." They operate in a completely different sphere from the library. They are more like mentors from whom the library can learn. Generally, at the local level, most businesses are more than willing to share ideas with you because they want the local library to be successful simply because it is good for the community. However, you do have to be proactive in seeking them out and asking for their help.

▶ Idea

Identify an area of service that you would like to improve at your library. Do an audit of your downtown businesses to identify those which are outstanding at providing that service. Then, set up a conversation with the owner of the business, armed with a set of questions and the goal of learning as much as you can that might improve how your library operates. Does the business consciously try to be outstanding at providing that service? Why? How does the company's strategic planning address that service? How do staff people get trained around that service? What systems are in place to support great execution of that service? In turn, be prepared to share ideas about what your library does well (if the business owner is interested in discussing this) so that hopefully the conversation is one from which you both benefit.

LEARNING

Empower staff to immediately make those decisions that will improve the customer's experience. The goal at Gelato Fiasco is to make the customer leave the store completely happy and satisfied with his or her entire experience. The staff who work behind the counter serving gelato are empowered to make whatever decisions are necessary to ensure customer satisfaction throughout each individual's interaction with Gelato Fiasco. Josh believes that customers should leave the store saying, "That was fun!" His viewpoint is that the only standard for staff in the store is to "solve customer problems and solve them yourself." In a lean organization, there just are not enough managers around for customer service questions to be solved by a manager. This needs to be done at the point of contact with the customer and done quickly and well. The employees in the store are encouraged to think in terms of what they can do to build relationships with their customers. Said another way, the primary goal at Gelato Fiasco is what they call a relationship transaction; the secondary goal is a financial transaction.

▶ Implication

Train and empower library staff to solve customer problems themselves at the point of contact with the customer. I am hopeful that a lot of librarians will read this and think this is old news. However, for those libraries which do not already operate in this way, this is an exceptionally powerful tool. Library staff can immediately address issues when they occur without having to resort to finding a manager to address the problem. This means that the patrons get their issues addressed quickly (and who does not want that to happen?), and speed of service does a great deal to make people feel better about their concerns. Good marketers know that customers have a common desire (see "Ten Commandments of Great Customer Service," by Susan A. Friedmann, at http://marketing.about.com/od/relationshipmarketing/a/crmtopten.htm for the full article). It is not to get what they want, which might be what you would expect. Rather, the shared desire is to be listened to with respect and not to get passed from one person to another in an effort to solve (or avoid) a problem. When a library patron is told by a library employee that he or she cannot fix a problem but instead has to get the director, it diminishes that employee and it annoys the heck out of the library user, who just wants to get a situation fixed now so he or she can get on with life.

Other benefits to having staff who can make their own decisions are that it makes them feel more trusted and more a part of the library culture and gives them more ownership in how the library operates. They are expected to act like adults by using their own judgment in situations and not adhering to some rigid set of guidelines that might or might not be appropriate in a particular scenario.

▶ Ideas

Ask library patrons to come in to talk with library staff about how they perceive customer service at the library. Customer service comes and goes as a topic of interest at libraries. Everyone who works at a library knows that it is important and that we need to focus on it as a skill. However, a certain degree of eye rolling tends to happen when it is raised as a training need. One way to address this slightly jaded perspective is to hear from library customers themselves versus having library managers lecture library staff about this topic. It is much more powerful to get input directly from the people you serve every day. This could involve hosting an annual focus group with library users, or it could be done on a regular basis or around specific customer service topics and issues.

Ask staff to identify customer service opportunities that can be improved and ways to improve them. This seems like another simple idea, but how often do library employees get the opportunity to identify what they think are the customer service opportunities at the library and then address them? Again, this idea can be simple or detailed. You could make this a regular agenda item during a staff meeting. You could have a contest for the best customer service opportunity identified by a staff member. You could highlight ideas from staff at board meetings so that the library's leaders understand and support the topics.

Talk about customer service all the time so that people are continuously learning about how to improve it in your library. You cannot expect library employees to own customer service as their responsibility if it gets discussed only once a year during training or when it is not done correctly. Customer service needs to be a regular topic of conversation so that library staff are continuously learning about how they can do a better job at it. Make this topic part of every staff and board meeting. You can identify examples of great customer service or talk about situations where customer service could have been better. The point is to keep the concept out in front of your organization as a goal that everyone has to work toward and that everyone has a personal responsibility for executing. The more employees are empowered to own customer service, the more likely that it will be constantly demonstrated in your library.

LEARNING

A strong organizational culture can create an environment in which people enjoy spending time. I worked in the corporate world for fifteen years after getting a master's degree in business administration. At that time, corporations worked hard to develop a uniform culture in which everyone had to participate (whether or not you were interested in doing so). I did not like that environment and I hated having to conform. As a result, when I became a library director, I was determined that I was not going to ask anyone on my staff to become a corporate clone (not that I think most librarians would do this even if you paid them!). After talking to Josh I began to adjust my thinking (a little!). I am still not interested in asking librarians to fit into a uniform corporate culture. However, I am starting to see more value in creating an environment that is unique and special and that creates a strong sense of "I'm lucky to work here" in those who are employed in that place.

Josh spends a lot of time working to create a unique place to which people feel privileged to belong and at which they will have fun working. Based on what I have seen (and knowing how much people seek out the opportunity to work at his stores), I think he has found a way to do this that attracts rather than annoys employees. Josh told me he seeks to create "a folklore and mythology" about the business because he sees this as a useful tool for developing camaraderie among his employees and for retaining employees. He helps create this mythology by using special nomenclature for the Gelato Fiasco business, the systems that make the business run, and the employees who work there. For example, the factory where the gelato is produced is called the "flavor foundry." The people who work in his stores are called "gelato wizards." The leadership team is called "the castle." As he explained it, the idea is to create an environment that is a bit like working at a summer camp, an atmosphere that is fun and makes you feel like you are part of an in group because you share the same jokes and reference points. The employees of his stores feel like they are being let in on a secret that makes them feel part of something bigger than themselves.

Another thing that contributes to the strong organizational culture at Gelato Fiasco is the hiring process. People are hired to work at Gelato Fiasco only after they go through a careful interview process. Potential employees start by having an interview with a group of people versus just one person. This makes the interview harder in some ways, but also something of a rite of passage that everyone who works in the store goes through. In addition, everyone who wants to work in the store has to contact Gelato Fiasco after this first interview to indicate that he or she is interested in being hired. This process then becomes a second rite of passage so that anyone hired at the store immediately has a shared experience with anyone else hired at the store.

▶ Implication

Shared experiences and language can help create strong bonds between coworkers. Even as I wrote this I thought to myself, "Well, obviously!" However, it seems like in libraries this concept can be problematic. The report *Planning for 2015: The Recent History and Future Supply of Librarians*, developed for the American Library Association, found that in 2009, 41 percent of librarians were in their fifties (www.ala.org/research/sites/ala.org.research/files/content/librarystaffstats/recruitment/Librarians_supply_demog_analys.pdf). As people get older, they focus more on their own lives with family and friends away from the job and they tend to be more comfortable with themselves, more self-assured, and less in need of belonging to a group to help them define who they are. All of these things make them less inclined to see belonging to a work group as important. However, what is still an important lesson is that shared language, shared experiences, and shared values have the same end result of building bonds among employees, and those bonds are an important goal if you want to have a cohesive organization with employees who work well together and, just as important, enjoy being with one another.

▶ Ideas

Consider having regular library staff events that are not meetings but rather social occasions, but make the events self-directed by library staff. Before the groaning starts, think about this statement. Regular does not have to mean every week; it can mean twice a year. These events do not have to be the dreaded team-building events to which many librarians have been subjected and which many hate. Shared activities are much more effective if they are staff directed, based on their interests and energy. The event does not need to have anything to do with team building; it can be about stress management or healthy eating or reading different genres. The subject really does not matter as long as it puts people together in the same space so they spend some non-work-related time together.

Several examples of "culture creation" at Curtis Library have been very successful. A number of years ago, library employees were dealing with a lot of stress-related problems. The staff indicated that they would be interested in attending early morning (before the library opened) programs that provided help for stress management. We held a series of meditation classes and yoga classes that library staff could choose to attend or not, and many chose to attend. More recently, a group of library staff indicated that they wanted to participate in a community program designed to increase workplace wellness. They agreed to go to the meetings and volunteered to do the work and planning related to the program. One of the activities that came out of the program was a monthly "healthy lunch" get-together for staff. Anyone could sign up to participate, with the only requirement being that you bring something "healthy" for the shared lunch. Participation was good, and the people involved seem to enjoy talking about healthier ways of conducting their lives. No one felt compelled to participate, so the people who were there joined in because they wanted to do it. The lunch has now evolved to a breakfast get-together just to keep things interesting, and participation is still strong.

Celebrate the lives of library employees. This one can be tough. Anyone who has worked in an organization with more than one person has lived through many, many birthday cakes, baby showers, and so on.

At Curtis Library we do little to celebrate life events, partly because Mainers are private about their personal lives, partly because Mainers are modest about their accomplishments, and partly because I just cannot stand the idea of having to eat birthday cake every week! The challenge in situations like this is to find a new or different way of celebrating beyond the traditional cake (and when you have employees coming and going sixty-two hours a week at a library, it can be difficult to find a time for everyone to get together for the cake). This is something I still need to work at in my own library, but here are some potential, cakeless ways you might set the stage for a celebration that does not mandate participation:

- Create a page on your library's intranet (or if you want to keep it low tech, you could place a notebook in a shared employee space) called "Employee Celebrations and Brags," sort of an internal Facebook. Employees could post their own birthdays or talk about the spectacular doings of their kids or grandkids or put up pictures of their latest knitting projects, and so forth. This way the celebrations are self-driven, not employer mandated. Employees can share what they want to share and decide for themselves if they want to read and respond to what others share.
- Have one get-together a month to celebrate employee events. Hold the event at lunchtime (at the end of one shift and the beginning of the next shift) so that anyone interested in attending can do so. Have a "wall of celebration" in a shared employee space where employees can post what they are celebrating that month. The library can pay for the basics of a shared lunch or snack if that is possible, or, if not, it could be a potluck event for those interested in attending.

LEARNING

Develop a hiring process that is unique to the needs of your organization. Much of my conversation with Josh revolved around how to hire and keep quality employees. After someone is interviewed at Gelato Fiasco, the interviewee is told that he or she must (after twenty-four hours) get back to the interview committee to indicate an interest in continuing the hiring process. No one is hired until this step is taken. Apparently, a lot of interviewees leave the store wanting to say right away, "Yes, I'm interested." But, after twenty-four hours, 30 to 40 percent of the people interviewed do not make this call. This statistic amazes me, but it does a good job of pointing out the value of making employment an intentional activity on the part of potential employees. If someone is really interested in working at Gelato Fiasco, he or she will jump this hurdle. And, since Josh only wants people who want to be in his store, this works out beautifully. Josh considers a job at Gelato Fiasco to be an opportunity for anyone who applies, and he wants employees who apply to feel the same way.

Another point that came up was that while interviewing employees, Josh consciously seeks people who have what he calls the "hospitality quotient"—those people who love to make other people happy and who enjoy helping people. He develops interview questions designed to highlight this characteristic and weed out those folks who do not think and act this way.

▶ Implication

Take the interview process very seriously and seek out excellence. I like that Josh sees interviewing and hiring employees as a core business activity. He knows exactly what he wants in the employees in his shops, he knows what he needs to be successful, and he is not willing to settle for good enough. People do not get hired for a job at Gelato Fiasco because they have worked in other jobs in his stores for a long time. They get a job because they are the right type of person for the job. I also like that Josh has developed a hiring process unique to Gelato Fiasco that helps create a unique culture. He does not use standardized questions in one-on-one interviews. Rather, he does group interviews, he asks the questions that will identify good employees for Gelato Fiasco, and he seeks out individuals who are proactive enough to tell him that, yes, they do want this job. As a result, in a business that would normally have high employee turnover, he has college students come back year after year to work in his store.

▶ Idea

Develop an interview process that is unique to your library and then do not hire a person unless he or she meets or exceeds your expectations. Hopefully, each person's job description in your library already defines what skills you want in that job. If you do not have carefully detailed job descriptions, writing them should be your first goal. Do not be afraid to use descriptive, fun language. If you need a "tech wizard," say that in the job description. The language that you use helps describe what you expect from that employee, and it also makes it clear that, as an organization, you do not take yourselves too seriously and you know how to have some fun.

When you need to hire for a position, look at the job description and make sure it reflects what you want the person in that job to do. Then, start considering how you can determine in an interview process whether the person being interviewed has those skills. Do not be afraid of being different in your approach to this process (although obviously you need to have a legal and appropriate process), and do not ever hire someone because he or she is good enough. Just because someone has worked in the library for years does not mean that person is the right person for a different job. In fact, I suggest that you use the same hiring and interviewing process that people outside the library go through for anyone who works in the library and wants to be hired for an open position. This is a positive for both the internal candidate and the library. If the internal candidate gets hired, both that individual and the library can be comfortable knowing that the person was truly the right person for the job.

Here are some examples of how you can develop a hiring process to find the right employee for your library: If you want to hire someone with initiative, try the Gelato Fiasco technique of having the person get back to you twenty-four hours after the interview to indicate an interest in moving forward. If you need someone who can do presentations, ask the person to give a presentation to the interview committee. If you want a librarian who has great customer service experience, ask "What if . . . ?" or "How would you manage . . . ?" questions during the interview. Do not be afraid to put a new hire on a ninety-day probationary period to see if that person is really right for the job. Bottom line: it is your library and you need to have a process that will do everything possible to guarantee the absolute best employees are working there.

LEARNING

If you are not serving the customer, why are you here? Josh considers every single job in his organization a customer service job. If it is not a direct customer service position (like serving gelato out front), then it is an indirect customer service position because it supports those on the front line. Everyone who works at Gelato Fiasco is expected to look at customer service as their primary responsibility. If they do not, then they do not stay in the organization. This ethic applies to the two business owners, to the bookkeeper, to the gelato servers, to the people who make the gelato. Everyone knows that this ethic is core to the organization and the driver for everything that happens.

► Implication

Everyone who works in a library should understand that they are there to serve the customer. Some jobs in a library do not seem to have any direct customer service focus, such as bookkeepers, administrative assistants, librarians who do not work on public service desks, and custodians. However, every one of these positions has internal customers even if it does not serve external customers directly. Everyone in the library needs to understand who their customers are and how they need to perform in their job to meet the needs of those customers.

► Idea

Ask every person in the library to define how his or her job is customer service oriented. Include this statement in the employee's job description, and each year ask that person to define how he or she will improve customer service. By making this a self-defined goal, there is a much greater likelihood that it will be real to the employee. Including customer service in yearly goal setting will help reinforce the message that customer service is critical to the library and a part of every single person's job at the library.

Make customer service part of your library's ongoing conversation. My library talks about customer service but not regularly. We do it when a customer service issue has occurred and we need to hash out as a library the right way of addressing that issue. I would like to change this and make customer service the core of everything we do at the library. How? One way is to develop a mantra to make sure library patrons are the center of what we do. So, the mantra might be something as simple as regularly asking, "What is right for the library's patrons?" or "Is that right for us or the patrons or both?" The mantra serves as a small "poke" to remind us about what is important. It also keeps what is important in front of us on a regular basis.

LEARNING

Use technology, but do not let it use you. It became very clear during the course of my conversation with Josh that technology is an important component of how he runs his business. He uses his cell phone to take pictures of things that give him ideas for his business, to stay in touch with his employees, and to check daily reports. He can log in to his cash register with his phone to see what is happening in the store in terms of sales. He works consciously to balance his inclination to manage by his intuition with an effort to manage by data. However, technology is not allowed to have an impact on customer service or any other part of customer and/or store operations. If a staff member is on his or her phone while working out front scooping gelato, he or she is fired. Technology has its place, but it does not run the place.

▶ Implication

Technology should be used to provide critical data and support for decision making. Libraries are moving rapidly to meet the technology needs of their patrons, from offering Nooks loaded with e-books, to providing digital projectors for use by library patrons, to teaching community members how to use Raspberry Pi (a credit-card-sized, single-board computer used to teach basic computer science). However, there is opportunity to do much, much more, using technology behind the scenes to help develop, plan, and evaluate the work that gets done to make the library run and provide services for the community.

Because funding is generally a struggle for most libraries, library employees frequently get stuck with old computers, very old servers, and second- or third-generation consumer technologies. They are experts at making do with what they have and able to accomplish what are frankly miracles with the aged technology they use. However, after talking with Josh, I think it is critical that libraries start to turn this paradigm on its head. Instead of library staff using technology until it falls apart from age, libraries need to put themselves on the cutting edge of consumer technologies and find ways to fund the purchase of those technologies on a regular basis, even if it means taking money away from the purchase of books. Why is this so important? There are two reasons. First, a vital role for libraries today is leading their communities through the labyrinth that is today's technology environment and they cannot do that unless librarians are experts at the technology themselves. Second, libraries need to start availing themselves of the benefits of technology to help librarians evaluate their work and today's technology can do that. But, librarians cannot do any of this with old, out-of-date equipment and no training in the newest technologies.

▶ Idea

Find the funding (grants, donors, tax support—whatever it takes) to equip library staff with one form of cutting-edge (versus leftover) consumer technology. Then, get them the training so that can use this technology to collect and analyze data about library programs, events, and services. This might mean buying all of the librarians on your staff iPads or cell phones that they can then use to do in-the-moment evaluation of library programs. It will mean reinforcing through training the value of data and how that data can be used in a positive way in the library. Make this process as transparent as possible. Set up central collection sites for the information being gathered so that everyone can look at and understand the data. In open staff forums, talk about how that information can be used to make decisions so that everyone understands its value. Ask for input from staff about the best ways to record and collect the information involved. Share what you discover with your leadership and funders and community. The more that people understand why (expensive) technology benefits the services they get from the library, the more likely they will be to support this type of spending.

LEARNING

"A library is a quiet space without distractions." During our discussion, I asked Josh if he used the library and, if so, how. I was surprised at his answer. About once a month, Josh calls the library to reserve for an entire day one of the study rooms that we have available for the community. He turns off his phone and spends the day reading and focusing on expanding his management skills. He views this as a productive day for his benefit only. He focuses on completing projects that are difficult to get done and reading that expands his professional expertise. He invariably comes back from these days with a body of work that would be difficult to accomplish any other way.

▶ Implication

Keep the old while you develop the new. Josh is in his early thirties, yet he wants to use the library in a very traditional way. He sees the library as a quiet place where he can get a lot of work done. Libraries struggle to build awareness about all of the new things they are doing to remain relevant. It may be that while libraries have been focused in that direction, they have lost an opportunity by not also promoting traditional library services. Why not keep talking about books and quiet spaces for studying even while starting to talk about e-books and community spaces and interactive learning? There will always be people who want and use the conventional components of the library, and we need to make sure that we do not lose sight of their needs in our rush to develop the newest services.

▶ Idea

Identify one thing in the traditional sphere of library services that your library does extremely well. Talk about it, remind people that you have it, and provide suggestions about why it is still relevant in today's world. One example might be to promote to small businesses that the library has the quiet space to let them do the type of reflective work that Josh does at the library. Or, you might remind people that the business books in the library can be an extension of their own business book collection. Or, make sure people know that they can reserve a meeting room at the library and have their yearly business meeting there. None of these is a new library service (quiet, books, community space), but each has real value, especially in today's noisy, busy, digital world. You just need to remind people that these services still exist at the library.

LEARNING

A librarian is a library's best asset, but not everyone has contact with a librarian. The last questions I asked Josh were if he had any ideas about what the Curtis Library could do differently or better and what did he think of the customer service provided by the librarians (since that topic had been the focus of so much of our discussion). I had been so busy being happy that someone his age uses the library that his next comment caught me by surprise. He said that he has almost no interaction with the librarians or other library staff, even though he is in the library regularly, so he could not give me any real feedback about the librarians' customer service skills. Josh reserves a room at the library on a monthly basis to do work for his business, and he uses the library's collection of business books to augment what he has in his own library. Yet, he rarely if ever uses the services of a librarian because he knows how to find what he wants on his own. In fact, if anything, Josh uses the library as a way of giving himself "alone" time for thinking and planning. He does not want to talk to the librarians and he does not need their help.

▶ Implication

Because self-service is an accepted part of our culture, many people may use the library without ever talking to a librarian or other employee. Your community may not understand or care that your library's best resource is its employees because they may never interact with the library staff. If a library user has no or minimal interaction with staff members, does the user still think that he or she is getting good customer service? Are the library employees and the library building providing good customer service? By that I mean the inanimate parts of your library (information on paper, signage, furniture, equipment, technology, Wi-Fi, rooms, copiers, etc.) must all provide good customer service. Those inanimate objects may be the only points of interaction for a patron at your library. If they fail to deliver, then that patron will think the library delivers poor customer service, even though the patron never talked to a single person at the library. Poor customer service results from not just a surly or unhelpful employee. It also can happen when furniture is broken, a piece of equipment does not work, signage is not clear, or the online room reservation system does not work.

▶ Ideas

Walk through your library and do an audit of all the inanimate things that provide customer service in your library. Look at everything from the perspective of a customer who has just walked into your library for the first time, needs to use your resources, but does not want to interact with a staff member. Identify what works perfectly without the need for any human interaction. Are library signs effective in helping people navigate your building without the need to ask directions? Can people figure out how to use copiers without asking a staff person to help them? Can patrons find the catalog computers and figure out how to use them without asking for help? Identify problem areas and develop teams that will "walk like a customer" with the goal of making recommendations for fixing the problems identified. Finally, recruit several community members to walk through your library and test your fixes.

If you have a building manager or regular custodian, ask this person to walk through the library each day and identify anything that is broken or out of place or not right. You can never have too many eyes searching out problems like this. You can also be sure that if you do not find these issues, your library users will find them for you. Staff should also participate in this process. Have one page on your staff intranet on which staff can identify a building issue that they have discovered. When that issue is resolved, post a note on the intranet so that everyone can see what has been resolved. Many eyes can help keep a big building looking its best.

Make sure that your virtual library is as customer service oriented as your brick-and-mortar library. Libraries have worked hard to develop usable websites that provide a great deal of information. However, even though use of these websites is generally self-service, they are not always customer focused. They become instead a dumping ground for all of the information that librarians think customers might ever need or massive bulletin boards that tell the community everything happening at the library. We put unedited videos of author talks on our websites. We ask our website users to click two or three or four times to get to the information they need. We forget that our websites, because they are self-service, need to be even easier to navigate than a trip to the physical library. The days of being a cutting-edge library simply because you have a website are over. Today, our websites need to be as good or even better at customer service than what we provide in our buildings.

If you are not sure if your library's website is customer focused, ask your customers what they think. Leave surveys in your computer lab. Put questionnaires on the opening page for using your library's Wi-Fi. Hold a focus group. Use Google Analytics to see what the statistics say about how many people use which pages on your website. However you choose to do it, get an understanding of what your customers use and do not use on your website. Simplify or eliminate those pages (no matter how great you think they are!) that are not being used or start working to increase awareness among library users about those pages so they will start using them. Think about your website as a way for you to provide services to your library users rather than using it to tell your users what you have. Look at commercial websites and see what they do. Today's standards for websites are being set by businesses, and we need to compete at that level of simplicity, customer service, and value to the customer.

• THE BIG IDEAS FROM THIS INTERVIEW •

Talking to Josh was my first foray into the "gray space" between organizations. Were there transformational ideas in that gray space? Yes, he shared thinking that has the potential to change how libraries operate. The first learning with that potential is the "Test, test, test—and fail quickly" concept. I know this is how entrepreneurs have always operated. However, it is truly different for librarians because we have always focused on making programs, products, and services perfect before we implement them. Using this concept could liberate how libraries operate in so many ways. Librarians can try out more ideas, we can spend less time and energy trying to reach perfection, and we can dramatically increase our ability to discover new ways of running our libraries in short periods of time. This means we can figure out how to stay relevant and meet the needs of our community without spending huge sums of money.

I also think that the learning "Library employees are a library's best asset, but not everyone has contact with a librarian" has the potential to be transformative because many library directors have not considered the impact of self-service on community perceptions about the library. Librarians are wonderful and smart, and most people come away from interactions with them raving about how great they are. Librarians are what make libraries the extraordinary institutions that they are today. But, what if someone spends a lot of time in the library and never talks to a librarian? How do we deliver outstanding customer service without having librarians involved? Addressing this question will certainly cause libraries to think differently about what customer service is.

Finally, learning that someone in his thirties still thinks that "[a] library is a quiet space without distractions" and sees this as being a good thing was certainly transformative to me. I spend so much time thinking about new programs to develop and new ways to run the library that I do not stop to consider how many people still appreciate and want some of the most traditional resources a library can provide, like a quiet space. It helped me understand that there really does need to be a balance between the old and the new in a library because, at least right now, community members want both.

• SUMMARY OF WHAT I LEARNED •

- Test, test, test—and fail quickly.
- Libraries and businesses can be pursuing the same goals, giving libraries the chance to learn from the businesses.
- Empower staff to immediately make those decisions that will improve the customer's experience.
- A strong organizational culture can create an environment in which people enjoy spending time.
- Develop a hiring process that is unique to the needs of your organization.
- If you are not serving the customer, why are you here?
- Use technology, but do not let it use you.
- "A library is a quiet space without distractions."
- A librarian is a library's best asset, but not everyone has contact with a librarian.

• RESOURCES •

Entrepreneur section, Forbes.com, www.forbes.com/entrepreneurs

Entrepreneur.com (Start, run, and grow your business), www.entrepreneur.com

The Lean Startup: How Today's Entrepreneurs Use Continuous Innovation to Create Radically Successful Businesses, by Eric Reiss (Crown Business, 2011)

• INTERVIEW QUESTIONS •

What do you think it takes to keep an organization flexible and nimble, the way it was when it was a start-up?

What do you think are the most important things an organization can do if it wants to be entrepreneurial (comfortable with risk taking in order to drive reward)?

Do you have processes in place to keep Gelato Fiasco entrepreneurial? If so, what are they?

Do you seek out advice and input from others about how to do business? If so, who and how? Does your advice always come from within your own industry?

How do you know when you are being a successful entrepreneur?

Do you consider yourself to be a risk taker? How do you define risk taking?

Do you think people can learn to be risk takers and, if so, how?

How do you build an organization that embraces or is at least comfortable with risk taking?

How do you define a business "failure"? When something fails in your organization, how do you deal with it?

Do you use data in your decision making or do you make decisions on the fly? Or both?

How do you get the ideas for new products or services?

Do you have a pipeline of ideas for new products/services? Do you have processes in place to support the development of those ideas? What are they?

Do you look for customer input about new ideas or do you just roll them out and see what happens?

How long do you stick with a new product or service before you decide it is not going to work?

Is your store a different "product" from your ice cream? Do you market your store or your product or both?

What kind of people do you try to hire? Can you identify four or five words that would describe the majority of your employees?

What processes do you have in place to help you hire the type of people that you want in your company?

How much do you depend on your gut instincts, how much on input from your staff and customers, and how much on data when it comes to making business decisions?

How does "leadership" happen in your organization? Are you two the leaders or are there other, nontraditional leaders?

How are decisions made?

Do you encourage input from your staff and, if so, how do
you get that input?

How do you set a common direction for your organization?

How do you ensure that you can jump on opportunities
quickly when they happen?

How do you build an organization that can move quickly?

If you were to start Gelato Fiasco over again, what would you
do differently?

If you were running Curtis Library, what changes would you
make in how the library does business?

3

CREATIVITY

WALTER BRIGGS
Briggs Advertising

• WHY THIS TOPIC •

Creativity is a topic of endless fascination to me. Creative people look at the world with open, unbiased eyes. They are willing to try out new ideas, they are comfortable with ambiguity, and they love to learn. If there was ever a time when libraries and librarians needed to be creative, it is now. Our organizations are evolving at a breathtaking pace into a new type of community institution, and yet it never feels like we are moving fast enough. We are trying to find new ways of curating our collections, serving our communities, educating ourselves, and evolving as a profession, all while we continue to maintain the traditional library alongside the new library. Creativity is one of the most important tools that will help us do all of this, manage through the next ten years, and define a new type of library that will be an outstanding community resource.

• WHY THIS ORGANIZATION •

Curtis Memorial Library hired Briggs Advertising several years ago to help develop a new brand for the library. During this process it became clear that Briggs understood the power of a carefully crafted brand and had the creativity to develop something special for Curtis Library. Their work process, the brand that they produced for Curtis Library, and their approach to developing multiple sub-brands for the library were all among the most creative work methodologies that I have encountered. Therefore, when I decided that creativity was one of the subjects on which I wanted to focus for this book, I immediately set up time to talk with Walter Briggs, owner of the company. Our discussion about creativity was wide-ranging and theoretical, but I could also immediately see how to incorporate some of what he discussed into the work process at Curtis Library. My primary goal for this interview was to understand how to put the people and processes in place in an organization so as to encourage a culture that could produce quality, creative products and service for customers day after day, year after year.

• INSIGHTS FROM THIS INTERVIEW •

LEARNING

At its core, creativity is problem solving. We talked a great deal about the definition of creativity. Walter views creativity as the ability to solve problems. He does not think creativity is a magical skill that you either are born with or not, which was one of the questions I put to him. Rather, he views creativity as the ability to identify an issue and then determine options for addressing or resolving the issue. Problem solving can be taught. Therefore, creativity can be taught.

We talked about some of the skills that, once learned, can help make people more creative. The ability to do research by evaluating a great deal of information and distilling out the most important parts is very important. Curiosity and an interest in constantly learning new things are also core components of being creative. If you are curious, you are interested in finding out the answers to problems, and if you like to learn, you are always willing to explore new paths of thinking and unusual perspectives.

▶ Implication

People can learn the skills needed to be good problem solvers, so they can also learn to be creative. The skills needed to be a good problem solver are taught as part of the process of learning critical thinking. Step one, identify the problem. Step two, learn as much as you can about the problem. Step three, brainstorm as many different solutions as possible. Step four, analyze the potential solutions and identify the ones that you are going to implement. Step five, implement the solution and collect data about the results. Once learned, this process can (and should) be applied to any question or problem that comes up in an organization. By understanding how to solve problems, anyone can become more creative because they will have a structure and a process to help them find a wide range of answers to problems.

▶ Idea

Train library employees in the process of critical thinking so that everyone who works in the library can apply it to the range of issues that comes up in their day-to-day jobs. This training does not require bringing in an expert at great expense; it can be self-taught through the many available books and articles about the problem-solving process. The training can be as simple as identifying one reading to explain each step of problem solving and then having regular staff discussions about the learning derived from the reading and how it might be applied in the library. The more difficult and more important part of this idea is that once employees understand the process of problem solving and how it might be used in the library, you need to start empowering them to do this. The best way I know to do this is to begin asking them to solve problems. This requires willingness on the part of library leadership to step back and let others address issues. As people come to understand that they are being encouraged to find answers to problems, creativity will start to become evident very quickly.

▶ LEARNING

Just as creativity is problem solving, it is also resilience, meaning that creative people can fail, pick themselves up from that failure, and learn from what happened. Failure can have positive consequences when learning comes from it. Having resilience means that instead of letting failure knock you down so that you do not get up again, you use failure to evaluate what you have done and define what did and did not work so that you try again with hopefully different outcomes. You are re-silient because you spring back and try again. I heard this concept over and over from different people throughout the process of writ-ing this book. If you want to have the best, most creative organiza-tion, then you must be willing to make mistakes, learn from the mistakes, try again, and hopefully arrive at better solutions.

▶ Implication

A creative library is one that is able to process failure, learn from it, and try again. A creative organization does not see failure as a negative thing that must be avoided at all costs. Rather, failure is part of the creative (problem-solving) process. To arrive at new ideas and new ways of operating, an organization has to experiment and failure is an inevi-table part of experimentation. When failure is an accepted and nor-mal part of running a library that is used as a tool for learning, libraries will become more willing to try and fail versus producing something only when it is perfect (and how often does perfection happen?). The result of this perspective is that many more new ideas are generated and tried. The end product is more creativity and in-novation than when the goal is an absolute, guaranteed success the first time out of the gate.

One of the biggest obstacles to libraries' absorbing and using this implication is the very normal inclination of people to think that if an idea was tried once and it failed, then the idea will never work and should not be considered again, ever. I have heard myself say something to this effect at one point or another in my career as a library director, and I have had to catch myself, slow down, and con-sciously think about what is different now that might make a formerly unsuccessful idea be successful. If you find yourself saying, "That won't work; we tried it in the past and it failed," or you hear library employees saying something similar, slow down and think for a moment. Is there anything new that might change the outcome? What did we learn from the past failure that makes it more likely this will be successful now? Ask those questions. They are very helpful in stopping a knee-jerk reaction that could dramatically limit your creative output.

▶ Ideas

Take the idea of failure out of the closet and make it part of the daily conversation at your library. If you need to find another word for failure that makes it easier to discuss, then do it. Whatever you call it, the goal is to make the idea of not achieving perfect success a normal, commonplace, and acceptable discussion. At staff meetings, talk about experiments that were tried and did not work. In retrospect, what would you differently? What did you learn? Examine new initiatives critically when you have board meetings and identify what you learned. By talking about failure and learning in an open and positive way, you make it okay for things not to work and more likely that critical thinking will take place to ensure that learning happens. The more that these discussions happen, the less likely that libraries will get bogged down in the mentality of not doing something until it can be done perfectly.

If you are a leader in your library, be willing to step back and let things happen even if you are not sure the suggested solution will work. If you as a leader can demonstrate your belief in the capabilities of library staff by letting them "do their thing," then they will do their thing, learn from it, take pride in it, and be willing to do it again. Should you do this even if you think failure is imminent? If the failure will not destroy the organization, my perspective is that, yes, you should let it happen. Do not forget that you could also be wrong. If people do not fail, they will never get over their fear of failure and they will never be willing to try for the big, crazy (and ultimately wonderful) ideas that can propel libraries so much further than the incremental, smaller wins that happen when they are not willing to risk failure.

I understand firsthand how hard it can be to be hands-off on a project when you are not sure what will happen. However, I have also seen how beautifully this can work. Curtis Library has a Facilities Committee that takes ownership for many aspects of how the library looks and feels to our patrons. At one point, the committee recommended to me that we put café chairs and tables in an atrium area of the library to give people a place to relax and chat. I did not like the idea because it seemed like it would create a big, empty space in the middle of the library that would become a noisy spot with no real purpose. I had a lot of discussions with the Facilities Committee team members about this and was open about expressing my concerns. However, I decided to step back and assume that we could learn from doing this regardless of the end result. I am very glad that I did. The tables and chairs have become a popular meeting space for people throughout the community. Seniors come in to chat after they have picked out their books to read. Day care providers use the space to give their kids lunch after they have visited the children's room. Businesspeople meet there. The atrium has become a hub for the community, and that was exactly what the Facilities Committee had hoped would happen. They were right, and I am learning to relax and trust their judgment. Trust is a core component of letting go and giving people the opportunities to make changes. Library leadership has to trust that library employees are smart and will find good answers, even if they are not exactly the answers that the leadership might have developed. Leaders also have to trust that if something does not work, the world will not come to an end and everyone can learn from the process. Library employees have to trust that their leadership will support them, regardless of whether the idea works. They also have to trust their own creativity and ability to solve problems. With trust going full circle within the library, this idea may be one of the most powerful that you will discover in this book.

LEARNING

There are no absolutes in a creative environment. In a creative environment, "No" and "That will never work" are not heard. Instead (and this also was expressed in multiple interviews for this book), in a creative environment you will hear things like, "I see how we might build on that idea" or "There are some ways we might use parts of that concept." In other words, there is possibility and opportunity in every idea. You just have to look for them and tease out the idea from the clutter that might surround it. There are no bad ideas, and everyone's input has value.

The other part of this learning is that in a creative environment, there is never just one answer to a problem. People who are good problem solvers will generate many potential answers to issues. They may all be good ideas, and each one of them may contribute something important in the long term. There are many ways to get to the desired end solution, and it may not be the one that a library director or manager develops. If you trust in your library employees' capabilities, then you will be willing to let them try their solutions.

▶ Implication

In a creative organization, there is value in the problem-solving process even when it does not lead to the answer because every idea has some potential. In brainstorming sessions, there is a period of time when everyone offers their ideas, and participants are not allowed to say why something will not work or why it is a bad idea. In a creative organization, the same concept holds true. Not every idea will be the perfect answer to a problem, but there is potential in every idea created. Two things happen when an organization values both the potential and the people who created the potential. A garden of ideas and creativity is created that may be harvested in the future for the organization, and because people feel valued for their creativity and problem solving, they will continue to try to be problem solvers.

▶ Idea

Develop a problem-solving pool for your library. Make the pool available to every member of your library so everyone can contribute. People can identify any problem that they need help addressing or that they see in the library. However, the person who identifies a problem to be solved becomes the owner of that problem. This means that the contributor must articulate at least one suggestion for addressing the problem before opening it up to the community. Once the problem is opened up, people can make a suggestion of their own or add to what others have already suggested. No one can say why an idea will or will not work or that it is not a good idea. Ultimately, the owner of the problem decides when there has been enough brainstorming and closes the conversation. This person also decides which contributed idea has the most value and takes the necessary steps to make it happen. All ideas generated can then go into a central repository because they might be useful for future situations at the library. Thus, over time, the library builds its own problem-solving file that becomes a useful organizational resource.

LEARNING

Creativity is a teachable skill. However, everyone learns differently, so the way that you learn creativity will vary depending on how you learn in general. The keys to learning creativity are a willingness to keep reaching and teaching yourself throughout your lifetime and always keeping a sense of curiosity about how the world works. If you enjoy reading, read as broadly as you can and try new types of literature. Challenge yourself by taking courses in new subject areas that have nothing to do with your profession. Ask people about their passions and learn what motivates them. Try something new that will stretch your capabilities and expand your comfort zone. All of these things will help make you more creative in your thought process and give you more tools to use as in problem solving.

▶ Implication

The opportunity for library employees to learn and grow should never end. Everyone who works in a library that expects creativity from its employees should be in a process of continuous learning regardless of their experience level or how long they have worked at that library. What is being learned and how it is being learned will vary for each person, but the point is that learning never stops. If library employees have worked at the same library for many years, the odds are that they know their jobs very well. When you know your job well and do it every day, it is often easy to slide into rote behavior, meaning that you act without thinking because you do not need to think to get the work done. Rote behavior is the opposite of creativity. Learning new skills is a great way to combat this because it interrupts the mindless behavior, increases the spectrum of work that you are able to manage, and gives you more ways to think about and find answers to situations that you encounter. If you are thinking about what you are doing, it is much more likely that you will apply your problem-solving (creativity) skills.

▶ Idea

Every library employee should have yearly goals to work toward achieving, and at least one of those goals should be learning related. A goal might be something as simple as reading two or three articles about customer service or listening to a particularly good podcast about customer relationships. Or, it might be as complicated as attending a series of seminars about adult literacy and how to support it in a community. The key point is that everyone in the library should be in a process of continuous learning. Does this idea apply to everyone in the library, including shelvers, part-time workers who staff the circulation desk, and those who work in a back room unpacking interlibrary loan requests? Yes, yes, and yes! I believe that the more repetitive a job is, the more that learning needs to happen to ensure that people are thinking and paying attention to what they are doing.

LEARNING

Valuing creativity is a starting point for building an organization that is creative. It is one thing to talk about creativity and why it is important. It is another to make it a part of the heart of an organization. I asked Walter how he would develop an organization that can be creative day after day, one in which creativity is part of the core of the organization. His response was very simple. You have to value creativity to build an organization that is creative. You value creativity by removing the barriers that keep people from being creative and by rewarding creativity when it happens. Removing barriers means teaching people how to solve problems and then giving them the space to do just that without trying to control the outcome. Rewarding creativity means that people are supported in their efforts to be creative, regardless of the outcome.

▶ Implication

If you want an organization to have creativity as part of its DNA, creativity should be identified as a core value that will be embraced by the entire organization. Creativity needs to be identified as something critically important to a library. Is it part of an organization's values statement? Is it included in job descriptions as a requisite of the job? Is there some measure of compensation tied to creativity and/or problem solving? Is there regular staff training about creativity and problem solving? Is creativity recognized in the work of staff? If creativity is not called out in strategic documents as being a core component of how your library operates, then creativity is not as valued as you think it is (or should be).

▶ Ideas

Do an audit of what your organization identifies as important in its values statement, strategic plan, job descriptions, and so forth. How are creativity and problem solving included in these documents? Have they been included or left out? Once you understand the history of how this value has been considered and its current role in the organization, you can start a library-wide discussion about creativity and problem solving and the role they should take in the library. The process of talking about these values will do a great deal to bring them to the organization's attention as critical components of organizational process.

   Train library employees about creativity, show them how to incorporate it into their jobs, and reward them for being creative. Bringing creativity and problem solving into the organization's awareness is important. However, you cannot expect people to start being creative if they have never been trained to be creative or to understand how problem solving results in creativity. Provide classes for library employees, and once they have started training, review job descriptions and incorporate the need to be creative in each person's position. It can be very difficult to include creativity as a skill in a job description because it means so many things and often people do not see it as part of their job. However, every job has some component that requires creativity. Start to include evaluation and compensation for creativity in job descriptions for every job in a library.

Ask library staff to identify organizations, or people, that they think are highly creative. Have a team conversation about why various organizations are creative and what they do that makes them that way. You might want to start the discussion by offering examples of companies that you think are creative and why and then segue to a discussion about creativity at your library. Are there ways that creativity is not being supported in the library? What might be done differently? Input from library staff is a great way to audit the degree to which creativity is an understood value for the library.

LEARNING

Groups are important for defining a problem, but the best ideas come from individual thinking. This was an interesting part of the conversation because it differed from what I had always assumed, which was that you get the best ideas from teams and group work. The discussion started from my asking about processes that are used to help develop creativity. Apparently, there are many different ways to develop creative thinking (more on this later). However, Walter's perspective was that the best creativity does not come from brainstorming or some other creative-thinking process. Rather, he thinks that while groups are important for identifying problems, the best creative ideas come from one person's thinking about the problem.

► Implication

Library employees need to have time to do unstructured thinking as part of their job responsibilities if they are expected to be creative and able to do outstanding problem solving. Library employees have very little quiet time in their day. If they are not on a service desk working with the public, they are working behind the scenes on programs, projects, or the library collection. They generally work in shared spaces with other library employees where it is very difficult to find quiet or privacy. If they want quiet, unstructured time to be creative, more often than not, they have to search for that at home or even out in the library. If libraries value creativity and problem solving, they need to determine how to support this work and provide librarians with the time and space that will enable them to get it done.

▶ Ideas

Provide library employees with paid "Google time" to do creative, unstructured work for the library. At Google, employees are given 20 percent of their time to apply to creative development. Most libraries would not be able to do this because they do not have enough staff or funding to free up that time. However, what if libraries provided even three hours a week for this work for those interested in doing this type of work? It would support creativity in the library but could be managed in terms of staffing coverage. If you choose to participate, then you could work on whatever creative project you wanted as long as it would ultimately benefit the community through the work of the library. The only caveat would be that you would ultimately report on what you did to library managers and the library board. I am sure not all library employees would take advantage of this because some would see it as more work. However, I think those who are interested in having a job that is creative would see this as a wonderful opportunity to try something different.

If providing a specific amount of time for creative development is not an option at your library, consider having a library equivalent to a tech company "hackathon." A hackathon is a programming marathon, followed by demonstrations and presentations and, sometimes, awards. Most libraries could shut their doors for one day a year. Interested employees could spend the morning of that day working together to brainstorm ideas around a concept that they want to address. In the afternoon, they could present their ideas to the library leadership to determine which ones will be executed.

Reserve private space in the library for use by library employees. I hear frequently about how difficult it is to think in a shared workspace, and I agree that it can be next to impossible. If this is an issue in your library, consider reserving a small space somewhere in the library for librarians who need to do quiet work. This would give them the privacy they need to concentrate and would demonstrate the library's commitment to the process of individual creativity. If you have a small library, consider reserving a corner for quiet work. If you have a board room that gets used only monthly for board meetings, consider making that the quiet workspace for employees. If demand for the room is heavy, set up a reservation system that limits its use to two-hour sessions.

Quiet workspace is something of value, not just to your employees, but also to the community. Today, quiet is a much desired, hard-to-find commodity. Do not forget that providing it as one of your library's traditional services will most likely be highly valued by your community.

LEARNING

A key component of creativity is a willingness to learn to think unconventionally. A lot of the tools that exist to support creative thinking are effective because they cause your thinking to veer off its normal track and make associations and connections that are new. New connections can lead to a different perspective about a problem that, in turn, can result in innovative solutions to the problem. Unconventional thinking can be learned with practice and desire. Be open to trying new books, food, music, and travel. Talk to people who do not work in your field and really think about what they do. Question assumptions when you find yourself making them. Does something really have to stay the same just because it has always been done that way?

▶ Implication

If thinking unconventionally and creatively is valuable to your library, help your employees get their creative mojo up and running. It is easy to get into a rut and not even realize it. Anyone who has been in the same job for more than a few years is likely to face this issue. We routinize our lives so that we do not have to think about every single thing that we do. It simplifies how we operate. The reverse side is that once we start approaching our jobs that way, we lose the tremendous value that thinking creatively and unconventionally can bring to our work. I think most librarians who fall into a rut know that they are there but are not quite sure how to get out of it.

To address this issue, libraries need to give their employees tools and processes to help them shake up their thinking. Here are some examples:

- One simple way to break out of a rut is to ask library employees to change their work space. If they have created a crowded mess in their cubes, designate one day specifically for cleaning, clearing, and consolidating what they have squeezed into their areas. If their work spaces are reasonably neat already, give them a morning and some funds to do a "remodel" of their area. This could be as simple as bringing in some plants or new prints for the walls or putting a coat of paint on everything. If everyone has the perfect work space already, have a Changing Spaces day during which everyone works in a different cube or space for one day. The goal here is to demonstrate to employees that they can change their thinking by something as simple as changing their work environment.

- Ask employees to bring their "passion" to work with them and share it with other staff during a shared meal. The process of talking about something that you love can ignite all sorts of energy. At the same time, learning something new is a wonderful way of developing new thought processes. Have a brown-bag lunch once a month to bring employees together to learn something new that has nothing to do with librarianship. Someone might teach the group how to knit. Another person might talk about writing poetry. One employee might talk about volunteering at the local homeless shelter. At the end of the lunch, the attendees can talk briefly about whether they got any ideas that they might use in the library.

- Provide a reading list for the librarians. We spend so much time as librarians helping other people find materials to read that I think sometimes we forget to nourish our own reading habits. Develop a "staff recommends for staff" reading list that includes both recreational and professional reading suggestions. When a librarian reads a book recommended by another librarian, suggest that they get together to talk about the reading. Nothing can break you out of a mental rut like reading a book that grabs your attention and forces you to look at the world differently!

Everyone gets in a rut and forgets how to think outside the box. By providing employees with different tools to reignite their creativity flame, you can help them get their unconventional thinking process restarted.

▶ Idea

Develop a "shadow day" with another library in your area. Working with another library (or several other libraries), set up a program for library employees to leave their library to shadow their peers in the other library. Then, host the other library's employees at your library. Seeing how other people do the same job that you do is a wonderful way of getting you to think in new directions. The person whom you shadow can help open up your mind to new ways of working and you can do the same for him or her. When I worked in Massachusetts, a group of library assistant directors developed a program called Me and My Shadow to do exactly this (the program won the American Library Association's 2007 H.W. Wilson Library Staff Development Grant, given to one library nationally each year). The program was very successful and had a high level of voluntary participation. What participants liked most was the chance to see how their peers found creative solutions to issues that they all faced. The program gave everyone new answers to old problems and at the same time helped reenergize their creative-thinking process. (If you are interested in learning more about the Me and My Shadow program, visit www.ir reverentlibrarian.com.)

LEARNING

There are many simple, easily accessible tools available to help develop creative thinking in an organization. Even companies that live creativity every day, like ad agencies, have a need for systems and processes that help them produce creative thinking. As Walter and I were talking, I looked around his office and immediately saw several types of creative-thinking aids, like the Creative Whack Pack. (The Creative Whack Pack provides sixty-four cards with a different strategy for approaching problem solving creatively. Developed in 1989, it is used by people across industries to help them "whack" themselves with a new way of thinking.) It was reassuring to see this tool and know that even people who live creativity every day use whatever tools they can to prompt new ways of considering problems and finding original answers.

▶ Implication

Libraries can make resources available to help train employees in creativity and problem solving for minimal cost. Creativity is one of those topics that scare people. It seems complicated and exclusive. However, literally thousands of tools are available to help organizations get past those fears and start being more creative, and many of them are free or low cost.

▶ Idea

Develop a finding aid for library employees that will guide them to different creativity training resources. Provide employees with time to explore these tools and develop a process for sharing their learning with all of your library employees. A finding aid will give employees the chance to explore as many opportunities as they want, allowing them to pick and choose for themselves the type of training that they like and from which they can best learn. If possible, libraries should provide access to some of the following tools at low or no cost:

- Consider purchasing a Creative Whack Pack for everyone who works in your library. The Creative Whack Pack provides new ways of looking at problems in the hope that jolting you out of your current perceptions will result in new solutions.

- Search for free or inexpensive apps that support creativity or problem solving. Some of them are just plain fun (e.g., Coffitivity, which sounds like a coffee shop, may work for those who are most creative in a busy environment).
- Search Google for "creative problem-solving tools." My first search produced over 1.3 million results.
- Visit Coursera.org for free courses on creative problem solving.
- Ask library employees to read a book that is in the library collection and then talk about it with other people who work at the library. Try *Inside the Box: A Proven System of Creativity for Breakthrough Results* by Drew Boyd and Jacob Goldenberg (Simon & Schuster, 2013) or *Play at Work: How Games Inspire Breakthrough Thinking*, by Adam L. Penenberg (Portfolio Hardcover, 2013).
- Give library employees a list of simple ways that they can boost creativity and ask them to add their own suggestions. Here are some simple ideas to get started:
  Stop watching television. Television kills creativity be-cause it does all the thinking for you.
  Take a twenty-minute walk. This will give your brain a break so it can come back to the issue at hand reinvigorated.
  Listen to music that you have never heard before.
  Try some kind of art or craft, whether it involves a crayon or finger painting or knitting or rug hooking. While your hands are working, your brain engages in new ways.

Identify a shared space on your intranet or in a staff room where employees can leave their thoughts and ideas about these resources, add to the "how to boost your creativity" list, and keep track of other resources as they come across them.

LEARNING

Part of being a creative organization is learning to let ideas "ferment." Often there is pressure in organizations to get to the right answer as quickly as possible. Brainstorming is done to find answers to specific questions or issues, and once the brainstorming is finished, the drive is to pick a direction. However, in a creative organization, there is a willingness to let ideas sit and ferment. The reason is that a core component of problem solving is the process of making connections between different elements of the issue at hand and the solutions that are being suggested. If some of those connections are missed, then it is likely that the solutions identified will not be as encompassing or powerful. Letting ideas sit so that the subconscious can work on them makes it much more likely that connections will not be missed and solutions will be richer and more refined.

▶ Implication

Libraries need to incorporate time for idea fermentation when they do brainstorming. I find that there is always a rush to find the right answer when brainstorming. We go through the process, see several good answers, and jump on those answers as the right ideas to pursue. Generally, we do not give ourselves the opportunity to put ideas to the side, let them sit for some time, and then go back to them. As a result, we may miss the truly transformational ideas.

▶ Idea

Make a forty-eight-hour cool-off period part of any library brainstorming sessions. After the forty-eight hours have passed, go back to the solutions that looked good at the end of the brainstorming session. Do they still look good? Have better ideas come to the surface or has someone built on one idea to come up with an improvement? As a group, talk about the difference in the quality of the pre- and post-cool-off ideas.

LEARNING

The biggest obstacle to the development of creative people is each person's own assumption that "I'm not creative." This discussion was at the end of our interview and seemed to be the perfect summary of everything we had discussed. The biggest obstacle to developing creative organizations is probably the fact that most people do not see themselves as creative. By defining creativity as the learnable skill of problem solving, everyone suddenly has the capability of "being creative." If people believe they have the potential to be creative, then they will be much more likely to give it a shot and see what happens.

▶ Implication

By changing how libraries define creativity, being creative becomes more accessible to every employee in the library. Librarians are problem solvers. People ask them for help in gathering information or identifying a good book to read. I know many librarians who would never describe themselves as "creative" but would be happy to tell you that they are good at solving problems. By changing how the library culture defines creativity, using language that works in the library culture, we have the opportunity to bring a lot more librarians into the fold of being creative. If every employee in the library is seen as having some component of his or her job tied to creativity and problem solving, then the library as a whole will benefit.

▶ Idea

Keep a list of examples of staff and/or volunteer creativity or problem solving at your library. Put the list in a location where everyone can see the list regularly. Make sure that what is defined as creative is broad so that employees start to understand that creativity can be learned. Ask staff members to include their own examples. Talk about the examples that people identify with the goal of gradually expanding the group's vision of what defines creativity.

• THE BIG IDEAS FROM THIS INTERVIEW •

The learning "At its core, creativity is problem solving" and the learning "Creativity is a teachable skill" are both very powerful. They indicate that creativity is a skill that can be learned versus the result of a genetic lottery. This, in turn, means that there is no reason why every library in the country cannot use creativity to find new ways of meeting the needs of their communities.

Another learning that ties in to the first two and is equally important is "A key component in creativity is a willingness to learn to think unconventionally." Thinking unconventionally in this context means that we, as library leaders, are open to the idea of thinking outside the norms of the profession to find ideas that have the potential to change how we do business.

• SUMMARY OF WHAT I LEARNED •

- At its core, creativity is problem solving.
- Just as creativity is problem solving, it is also resilience, meaning that creative people can fail, pick themselves up from that failure, and learn from what happened.
- There are no absolutes in a creative environment.
- Creativity is a teachable skill.
- Valuing creativity is a starting point for building an organization that is creative.
- Groups are important for defining a problem, but the best ideas come from individual thinking.
- A key component in creativity is a willingness to learn to think unconventionally.
- There are many simple, easily accessible tools available to help develop creative thinking in an organization.
- Part of being a creative organization is learning to let ideas "ferment."
- The biggest obstacle to the development of creative people is each person's own assumption that "I'm not creative."

• RESOURCES •

Creative Confidence: Unleashing the Creative Potential within Us All, by Tom Kelley and David Kelley (Crown Business, 2013)

"Creativity," TED Talks Topics section, TED.com, www.ted.
com/topics/creativity

"Eight Awesome Creative Thinking Techniques (Plus Tools),"
by Harry Gardiner, Koozai.com, July 16, 2013, www.koozai.
com/blog/search-marketing/content-marketing-seo/
eight-awesome-creative-thinking-techniques-plus-tools

"How to Be Creative," by Jonah Lehrer, *The Wall Street Journal*,
updated March 12, 2012, http://online.wsj.com/news/
articles/SB10001424052970203370604577265632205015846

• INTERVIEW QUESTIONS •

How do you build a culture of creativity and innovation?
What do you think are the most important things an
organization can do to encourage creativity?

How do you minimize the "fear of failure" (or fear of
rejection or fear of looking stupid) that is inherent in the
creative process?

How do you get people to talk and think about creativity?

Do you have processes to help you and your organization
learn from failures?

What mind-sets, qualities, or talents have you found to
characterize top creative people whom you most admire
and how does one cultivate these attributes in a staff?

How do you make sure you are hiring creative people?

Do you think it is possible to train people to be creative? If so,
how?

How do you encourage curiosity in an organization, assuming
that curiosity is a critical component of creativity?

What organizations do you think do an amazing job of being
creative?

Do you think breakthrough ideas are as important, more
important, or less important than continuous
improvement in an organization?

What tools (reading, technology, activities, etc.) would you
recommend to help encourage creativity in an organization?

What do you think about the idea of giving employees dabble time (like Google) to experiment and work on innovative projects of their own choosing?

What do you think are the biggest barriers to creativity in an organization and how they might be addressed?

How do you balance creative thinking, creative risk, and creative action in your organization?

What is the most important thing an innovative leader could or should do regularly to stay effective and fresh in his or her work?

Do you think creativity comes out of collaboration or out of individual thought processes?

What is the most important thing that you have learned about creativity and people?

What do you think the leaders of organizations need to do if they want to encourage a culture of creativity?

If you had ten minutes to talk with library directors about today's libraries, what would you tell them to do differently to promote creativity among their librarians?

4

THE EXTRAORDINARY IN THE ORDINARY

FRITZ GROBE
EepyBird

• WHY THIS TOPIC •

The concept of seeing the extraordinary in the ordinary fascinates me (and, yes, I do love a good makeover show on television!). There is so much mystery and intrigue in the concept of looking at something very basic and simple and suddenly discovering something beautiful or funny or exciting within it. Consider how absorbing butterflies are and how the transformation from a drab caterpillar into a monarch butterfly consistently enthralls those who watch it happen. I think of the library in the same way. Libraries are practical buildings primarily designed to hold books. However, when you examine what happens in a library, suddenly what seems an ordinary place is transformed into something extraordinary where community is built, ideas are shared, information is conveyed, stories are told, and opportunities for change and growth exist. Libraries perform this enchantment every day in many different ways. However, librarians struggle to find methods to communicate about our libraries in a way that makes people want to listen. I see a transformational opportunity in librarians learning to see better what is extraordinary in what we do and share in such a way that people cannot wait to hear what we have to say.

• WHY THIS ORGANIZATION •

EepyBird is a wondrous, totally unique combination of two "guys," Fritz Grobe and Stephen Voltz. Fritz is a professional juggler and Stephen is a lawyer. In case you do not already know, Fritz and Stephen are also known as "the Coke and Mentos guys." They are the ones who put Mentos candy into bottles of Diet Coke and by doing so unleashed an extravaganza of exploding soda that made for one of the most fun, creative, viral videos ever shown on YouTube (search for Extreme Mentos and Diet Coke). That video has now been seen over 100 million times!

Beyond producing videos that are exceptionally popular and fun (and writing books and producing TEDx talks), the EepyBird guys explore "how ordinary objects can do extraordinary things" and how this can be shared in a compelling, creative explosion that captures extraordinary levels of attention. My goal was to understand how the EepyBird team does this so that libraries might develop some of the same skills. Fritz Grobe is a Brunswick native who grew up going to Curtis Memorial Library and so, despite an extraordinarily busy schedule, was willing to chat with me about libraries. To learn more, I traveled to the woods of Maine to spend some time at their headquarters—the EepyBird mother ship.

• INSIGHTS FROM THIS INTERVIEW •

LEARNING

Learning to see what is extraordinary in the ordinary requires developing and examining many different ideas to develop your sense of sight. Fritz and Stephen did not wake up one morning and say out of the blue, "Let's put Mentos in bottles of Diet Coke and watch it spray out; that will be so cool and it is guaranteed that 100 million people will watch it on

YouTube!" Finding an idea that was creative and fun and different required a huge amount of time on their part doing brainstorming, playing with different ideas, testing, playing some more, testing some more, and brainstorming some more. They worked hard to learn how to see the potential in ideas and then went through a process to determine if that potential would result in a reality.

Fritz is (in addition to being part of the EepyBird team) a professional juggler. He explained to me that he looks at creativity from a circus or physical perspective. No one expects to learn how to be a juggler right away, so why would you expect to be able to identify extraordinarily creative ideas as soon as you try? Not finding the perfect creative idea as soon as you start looking does not mean that the idea is not there or that you are not creative enough to find it. It simply means that you need to spend the time on this process to identify many ideas and explore many options. You have to go through this process of reiteration because it gives your brain enough ammunition to start seeing connections between ideas and learning from that. Once those connections are identified, your brain will start to use them as a springboard to new connections and you will find yourself getting closer and closer to finding the elusive "extraordinary." Albert Einstein articulated this approach by saying, "It's not that I'm smart. I just stay with problems longer."

▶ Implication

Libraries need to understand that creative exploration is a numbers game; the more ideas they develop, the more likely they will find the most creative ideas. The EepyBird guys spend a great deal of time seeking out the creative ideas that might be embedded in ordinary objects like Post-it notes, Mentos and bottles of Diet Coke, and paper airplanes. They play with the objects, brainstorm about ideas, and then they play some more. They develop more ideas and then even more ideas because their assumption is that the more they explore, the more likely it is that the great ideas will come to the surface. One of Fritz's suggestions was that when you start brainstorming, set a quantitative goal and do not stop until you hit that number. It is so easy to hear an idea come up during brainstorming and immediately think,

"That's the answer!" and then get complacent about going any further. Instead, the goal here is to keep generating and generating ideas, under the assumption that quantity will be the defining factor in discovering something unusual and extraordinary.

▶ Ideas

Teach librarians the elements of creative ideation to help them understand why it requires time, work, and the willingness to stick to it. Courses about creativity and creative exploration are now available on Lynda.com, a website that provides members with access to a large quantity of online video tutorials on a wide range of subjects. There are MOOCs (massive open online courses) available on creativity at websites such as Udemy.com or Coursera.org. At the very simplest level, a library can give library employees the time regularly to read blogs centered on creative development or to listen to TED talks, which, at their core, are all about creativity. Depending on a library's funding, I suggest making as many of these types of tools as possible available to library employees before starting the process of creative ideation. The more participants understand how the process works, the more they will be willing to work at developing a pool of ideas.

Provide at least a once-a-year opportunity for all library staff to participate in a creative exercise. It is important to exercise any skill in order to improve it. Hold a once-a-year program for library staff during which teams present their best story about what the library does that is extraordinary. Give the winners the opportunity to work with a professional videographer to develop a story about that service and then share the video online. The goal is to find opportunities for all staff members to get a chance to stretch their creative muscles and to share what they see as being extraordinary in the library. The winners also get the bragging rights for producing a professional video, and the library gets the opportunity to produce what will hopefully be a viral video.

LEARNING

If you set out to be brilliant, you will fail. I was interested in defining the process of creative development and how EepyBird discovers such wonderfully fun, silly ideas as dropping Mentos into Diet Coke. Fritz's response was simple. Do not start out intending to develop an idea that will result in a video that 100 million people will watch. That goal is too overwhelming, and most people will freeze at the start of the process. Instead, Fritz indicated that it is much easier to find those ideas which come out of brainstorming that are intriguing and have some small element of interest (i.e., "I think I see something extraordinary in that idea, but I can't quite figure it out yet") that you would like to pursue. Keep at it and keep at it until you become "the expert" at the idea that you have pursued, and in that process you will figure out if there is an awesome idea there waiting to be discovered.

When I looked at some of the EepyBird videos on YouTube, it became clear how serious they were about the need to experiment and play to become experts about a subject. Their Diet Coke and Mentos video did not reach its ultimate level of creativity (and fun) until experiment number 137! By that point, they really had learned everything there was to know about Diet Coke and Mentos and figured out that there was a great, creative concept just waiting to be shared. I think this goes back to Fritz's point that it takes time and iteration for the brain to start to see the really cool, fun ideas, and you have to go through that process to get to extraordinary.

▶ Implication

Experimenting and playing are great tools for libraries seeking to increase their creativity quotient. It does not seem to matter whether you are trying to find a fun idea for a video or a creative way of capturing the attention of people in your community. When your goal as a library is to be creative and exciting, you need to be willing to spend time playing and experimenting with ideas to learn everything you can about them. Only by doing that can you start to find the extraordinary that might be hidden within the ordinary.

The sense of *play* that I am talking about here is like that of child's play. It is very focused and experimental but at the same time it is meant to be fun and enjoyable and a way of exploring the world. To participate in play, those involved in brainstorming and creative development must be willing to let go of their perception of what is appropriate behavior and instead be willing to step off the beaten path and try new ways of understanding. The concept of play coupled with exploration also helps make the iterative process more interesting.

▶ Ideas

Ask library employees to spend some time at a children's library program, watching how kids interact, play, and learn. The goal is to have library employees walk away from these sessions with an appreciation for the power of play and the extent to which it can drive creativity. A community journal could be established in which participating staff could jot their ideas and anything they learn so that everyone in the library could benefit from the learning process. Another way to do this might be to ask children's librarians to provide weekly suggestions for children's books that the whole staff can read and discuss. The goal again is to spur an appreciation of the power of play in driving creativity.

Ask library staff members to find one video on YouTube that they love. Play the videos at a staff meeting and ask staff members what makes them love a particular video. Talk about what makes the videos creative and entertaining. What role did experimenting and/or playing take in the process of making the videos? How might library staff learn from that to try their own ideas?

LEARNING

Regular positive reinforcement can help develop a constant flow of new ideas. As Fritz and I talked, it became clear that when Fritz worked on a team with other people, if they took the time and mental energy to share an idea, then Fritz was going to value that idea and their initiative in producing it. It was very important to him that he did not say, "I don't like this idea" or "Here is the problem with this idea" because that will shut down new ideas very quickly and his goal was to produce as many ideas as possible. Bottom line: he felt very strongly that more positive reinforcement will equal more ideas, and more ideas will equal more creativity.

▶ Implication

Libraries need many ideas to end up with the great ideas, so they need to find a way of encouraging and supporting a steady stream of idea input. It is great to get new ideas about how to get the work done at a library. However, I find that often the ideas do not get proposed until a very specific question is asked. There is very little of the "Here's a good idea" on the day-to-day level. Perhaps one of the reasons why is that there is no process in place to capture ideas when they come up and so they come into staff's brains and then go right back out again in the pressure of day-to-day work. Also, in the hustle of a busy day, it really can be difficult to stop, find a pen and paper, and go into a quiet corner to write down an idea.

▶ Ideas

Set up a central collection point via e-mail or website for new ideas. Encourage everyone on the library staff, on the library board, and among library volunteers to contribute ideas electronically as they discover them. This should reduce the likelihood that people will not have time to register ideas because, in today's library work environment, librarians are rarely ever far from at least one piece of technology (computer, laptop, telephone) that will let them record ideas. The ideas can be submitted anonymously if people wish. Clear expectations should be set for the "idea central" (e.g., just because an idea is submitted does not mean it will be implemented, but it does mean that it will be seen and considered by library management) to make sure people do not get disillusioned if their ideas are not implemented.

If an idea is pulled out of idea central and implemented, reward the staff member who proposed the idea. When I worked in business, one of the companies at which I was employed had a productivity program. Company employees could identify new and better ideas for running the business. If ideas were implemented, the employees who submitted the ideas were given points that they would collect and then spend for various rewards. Why not institute a similar program for creative ideas in a library? It would help reinforce the idea that creativity is critical and valued and that the employees who think and act in this way are critical and valued also.

LEARNING

The likelihood is high that if you are trying to make something better, then you will make it worse or even break it before you find a better way, but this is just part of the process. Fritz made this point in the context of a juggling routine. You are going to take something reliable and solid that has worked for you in the past, and to make it new and different, you are going to "mess" with it, make it unreliable, or even make it not work at all. Then, to fix it, you will need to develop a better way, so you may have to go through a lot of failures to get to the improvement that you want. And failure is okay as long as it leads to something better, meaning that you have learned something from the failure and applied that learning to come up with a new and better way of operating.

▶ Implication

If you are trying to find new and better ways of operating your library, you should expect things to blow up every now and again. Libraries have the reputation as being places of learning and education where everything is in its place and answers can always be found. This is all good. However, would it not be great if libraries could also be viewed as centers for creative chaos where experimentation, trying new things, and occasional creative explosions are also part of the norm? It would open up the library to new users and open up library staff to new ways of operating. It would make for a more vibrant organization because change would consistently be part of the environment. It would mean that the library could try out more ideas and programs and processes because failure would not be feared but would be valued as a tool for learning.

How do we change the culture of libraries to be more accepting of occasional explosions? It has to start at the top with the library's leadership. If an experiment blows up, the library director has to respond calmly and not start hunting people down as part of the blame game. At the same time, the library's board has to be comfortable with explosions and not punish the library director for such occurrences. High levels of communication about the experiments being planned and potential problems that could occur are also helpful in setting appropriate expectations and making sure that people do not expect too much from a new process or program. As stated elsewhere in this book, trust comes from people assuming that they are getting timely, correct information. Trust will take an organization a long way toward changing its comfort level with fluidity and ambiguity.

▶ Idea

Develop a process for analyzing "failure" so that you extrapolate learning rather than assign blame. This could be as simple as asking all library staff to answer the question (when reporting about a project) "What did not work, what did I learn from that, and what will I do differently moving forward?" The goal would be to institutionalize the process of learning from things that do not work and to take fear of failure and any stigma out of the process of creative development.

LEARNING

Creativity comes from a lack of ego. This concept comes from Fritz's theatre and circus background. In the theatre, the goal of creativity is not to promote one specific idea but to find the *right* idea. We talked a lot about ego and how it inserts itself into the creative process in organizations. Ego looks like people who talk in brainstorming sessions (about what in their experience has and has not worked). Ego looks like the need to advocate for one idea because it is the right idea (at least in the opinion of the speaker). Ego looks like the need to critique others' ideas to bolster one's self-image. Ego looks like the boss telling a subordinate why something will not work at a brainstorming session. Eliminating the self in the process of brainstorming and making the session's goal the production of as many ideas as possible (without evaluation) increases the likelihood that a truly creative and unique idea will ensue.

▶ Implication

When libraries start working on creative ideation, job titles need to be left at the door. This is particularly true in libraries where library directors are generally perceived as being at the top of the organizational hierarchy. If a director asserts that role during creative development, it can do a lot to kill anyone's interest in the free flow of ideas. If your library is going to do creative ideation, consider finding symbolic ways of equalizing everyone who participates or make the process of ideation "blind" in terms of who is participating.

▶ Idea

Develop a blind online forum for creative exploration. On a regular basis a problem is delivered to the forum. The problem might be an issue that needs to be resolved, or a methodology for doing work that needs to be reworked or transformed into something new, or an idea that someone might have about what is extraordinary in the library. Everyone in the library is given the opportunity to respond with ideas and all responses are anonymous. The goal is to generate a large pool of ideas that grows until the individual who posed the question finds an answer that works. Because there are no names attached to the ideation, the hierarchy of the library is eliminated and hopefully what is left are just good ideas.

LEARNING

Ideation and brainstorming need to be nurtured in a safe environment. A safe environment is one in which all ideas are nurtured and appreciated. It is very easy to shut down a new idea by saying why something will not work or why you cannot do it. It is much more difficult to listen to all ideas and look for the one that might help the overall process. The way Fritz expressed this, over and over, was that the creative development process needs to be additive versus reductive. You do not want to shoot down anything; you do want to explore every possibility that comes up. The process needs to be constructive, not destructive. During brainstorming, the goal should be quantity of ideas, not evaluation of ideas. Setting a target for the number of new ideas that you want to generate might help hammer this point home and make sure that people participating are producing new ideas, not evaluating the ones already identified.

▶ Implication

Libraries that engage in creative ideation need to ensure that the process is supportive, not evaluative. The people who participate in brainstorming need to feel like they can be crazy and off-the-wall with their ideas without being judged. It also needs to be clear that good ideas come from everywhere and an idea will not be critiqued because it did not originate from someone in the library profession. Finally, it is important that ideas not be thrown out just because they have been tried before in the past and did not work. There may be something in today's environment that will help the idea to succeed when in the past it did not.

▶ Idea

Before beginning brainstorming, agree to eliminate words and phrases that can shut down brainstorming. Some examples are "That won't work because . . ." or "I like that idea because . . ." or "In my experience, we've always done . . ." When people use such phrases, have them put a dollar in a jar to reinforce the need to eliminate negativity, advocacy, and ego from the process of brainstorming. This may seem like a somewhat silly process for a room full of adults, but it is one way of increasing awareness about the need to explore and expand versus narrow, eliminate, and shut down. It also can be useful because the group involved in brainstorming will start to self-police after this becomes an accepted part of brainstorming.

LEARNING

Hierarchy works against creativity because the social consequences of failure are greater. It is difficult to get people to leave behind their day-to-day roles and responsibilities and simply be creative. You may feel that being too creative in front of your boss will likely bring repercussions in some form or another, and those consequences (whatever they are) may be more than you are comfortable facing. A stratified group in which the positions of boss and underling are very clear roles has a much higher likelihood of lack of participation because the social consequences of failure are high.

▶ Implication

If people at all different levels in an organization participate in brainstorming, hierarchy needs to be left at the door. It is easy to say this and a lot harder to do. Library staff members are frequently uncomfortable saying what they think if the boss is sitting and listening and waiting for someone to mess up. The boss may be doing nothing to critique or evaluate an idea, but the perception that this is happening may still exist, so if the boss is going to be in the room with everyone else during brainstorming, this has to be addressed. There is a simple way to make this point. Once everyone has entered the room where the brainstorming will take place and taken a seat, the facilitator for the brainstorming session can ask everyone to stand up and change seats. Why is this helpful? Over time hierarchy quietly asserts itself in many ways, including seating. Very often you will find senior managers at one end of a table and everyone else at the other end of the table, as far away from the managers as they can get. By asking everyone to stand up and change seats, you are disrupting that almost unconscious assertion of hierarchy and putting everyone on a more equal footing.

▶ Ideas

Address immediately the fact that the boss is in the room and have that person verbalize his or her commitment to an open and equal process for everyone. This still will not get rid of everyone's concerns about social hierarchy, but having the boss articulate his or her commitment to the process will help. Of course, action speaks louder than words, so it is important for the boss to manage his or her own interactions during the brainstorming so that he or she is supporting rather than sabotaging the process.

Keep library directors out of brainstorming sessions. I know this is a tough one. I am a library director, and I really enjoy participating in brainstorming sessions and exploring for creative ideas. However, the director can insert his or her ideas at any time during the creative ideation process. The director does not have to be part of brainstorming, and if the group might be more creative without him or her, then why not give it a try and see what happens?

LEARNING

If you want to think about your brand in a nontraditional way, consider what the brand does versus what it is. This answer was off topic, but it was Fritz's response when I asked him how he would find a compelling way of telling the library's stories. If you tell the story about an organization and describe it, then people will understand the organization and what it does but they will likely not have any particularly strong emotion about it. However, if you tell the story about what *happens* at the organization and what people *do* there, there is more emotion and power because the listeners start to relate their own experiences with what they are hearing. They connect on a personal level. So, instead of a library being a place where you borrow books (which is very literally what a library is), the library becomes the place where opportunity is created through the exchange of ideas, information, creativity, and community (which is what the library does). The second articulation appeals to people's emotions and therefore has much more power to attract people and get their attention.

▶ Implication

Consider what the library does and market that versus what the library is (a building to house books). Libraries are excellent at developing and marketing lists of the books and resources and programs that are available at the library. These are all very helpful and appropriate for the people who already use the library. However, if we want to attract more people into the library as new users, we need to think about telling a story that will connect on a more emotional level, showing how the library can help people in the community find

ideas and information and resources that will help them manage
their lives.

▶ Idea

*As you spend time in the community that your library serves, keep a list of ways
that you think the library could do more to help meet the needs of the community.* I regularly come up with my own ideas, and I hear ideas from
people who love the library and people who are unhappy with the
library and have some ideas about how to fix it. Sometimes ideas are
things that can be taken care of immediately, sometimes they will
take a bit of time and planning, and sometimes they will involve
extensive research and resources. I write them all down, but I also
try to identify immediately if I think it is a short-, mid-, or long-term
idea. This helps me prioritize the ideas and to start figuring out a
timetable for the projects.

LEARNING

*Shoot videos that are like a conversation, and think about these videos as a gift
to another person.* Videos are easy to shoot. Effective videos that capture attention and get shared with a wider audience can be much
harder to develop. I asked Fritz if he had pointers about how to do
this because it is so rare to find a library video that really grabs your
attention. I am particularly interested in videos right now because
they are such a wonderful way of showing the extraordinary in the
ordinary. Fritz mentioned both of the points in this learning; shoot
videos as if they are a conversation that you are having with a person
inside the camera, by which he meant that you need to relax and
talk versus reading a script. Creating a video as if it is a gift to someone else was another wonderful way to think about video development (or any other tool that you are using to promote your library).
In essence, you want to produce a video that you would want to
watch, one that is fun and funny, intriguing, and so different that
you want to pass it on to your friends. Looking at marketing tools
through this lens (do I want to share this with my friends because it

is so different and fun?) is a great way to help you figure out if you have hit the mark with your videos.

▶ Implication

Libraries need to loosen up when developing videos. Videos produced by libraries always feel ultrascripted and are really not much fun. They seem to reflect all of the traditional perspectives about libraries and librarians (libraries are serious places and librarians are serious people, but we will try to loosen up a little if it means we can get you to listen to us). Sometimes they just present a list of services that the library provides ("I'm Mary the librarian and I would like to show you some of what we have available here at the John Smith Library"). What we all need to do is just relax a bit, find an intriguing idea for a video, have some fun, and shoot it.

▶ Idea

Watch the video produced by the Nashville Public Library on YouTube (search for Nashville Public Library all about the books). Library employees are shown covering the song "All About That Bass" by Meghan Trainor with their own version "All About the Books." As of November 2014, the video had gotten more than 164,200 views, which has to be a record for a public library video. I shared it with everyone I know. Why? It is fun and funny and the people in the video are just plain having a great time (but they still get across a great library message). You smile while you watch it, and when you are done, you watch it again. This video is a great example of finding the extraordinary in the ordinary. There is nothing extreme going on in the video, no pyrotechnics or craziness. There are ten people (and some puppets) sitting in a dark room, singing, and having a blast doing it. And suddenly the video morphs from something ordinary that you might show the librarian at the next desk into something extraordinary that more than 164,000 people have looked at. That's what we're talking about, people!

• THE BIG IDEAS FROM THIS INTERVIEW •

Much of what I ended up discussing with Fritz was about the process of creative development, how to brainstorm productively and how to explore a small idea to see if there is anything wonderful in it that might turn it into a big idea. It was a fun, interesting conversation that covered a lot of territory.

I think the learning "Learning to see what is extraordinary in the ordinary requires developing and examining many different ideas to develop your sense of sight" has the potential to be transformative for libraries because it supports the idea that creative development is a developed rather than intuitive skill that can be done by anyone who will put in the time and effort to learn.

Another learning that I think has transformative power for libraries is "Shoot videos that are like a conversation, and think about these videos as a gift to another person." Librarians have focused on being reputable, intelligent, and accurate, which is all good. However, sometimes we can do a better job of communicating if we can let go of the job of educating and informing and just concentrate on sharing our passion for what we are doing. There is a great deal of power in just having fun!

Finally, I love the learning "The likelihood is high that if you are trying to make something better, then you will make it worse or even break it before you find a better way, but this is just part of the process." I heard this same idea expressed in different ways throughout the interviews for this book, which tells me that the concept is important. If libraries are to be successful in redefining what they are and how they serve their communities, they need to experiment and explore. In that process, they will inevitably make mistakes and "break" things, and that is okay.

• SUMMARY OF WHAT I LEARNED •

- Learning to see what is extraordinary in the ordinary requires developing and examining many different ideas to develop your sense of sight.

- If you set out to be brilliant, you will fail.
- Regular positive reinforcement can help develop a constant flow of new ideas.
- The likelihood is high that if you are trying to make something better, then you will make it worse or even break it before you find a better way, but this is just part of the process.
- Creativity comes from a lack of ego.
- Ideation and brainstorming need to be nurtured in a safe environment.
- Hierarchy works against creativity because the social consequences of failure are greater.
- If you want to think about your brand in a nontraditional way, consider what the brand does versus what it is.
- Shoot videos that are like a conversation, and think about these videos as a gift to another person.

• RESOURCES •

CreatingMinds.org (Practical tools and wise quotes on all matters creative), www.creatingminds.org

"15 Creative Blogs and Sites for Innovation and Inspiration," by Amanda Lewan, Michipreneur.com, January 7, 2013, www.michipreneur.com/15-creative-blogs-and-sites-for-innovation-inspiration/

"How to Build Your Creative Confidence," by David Kelley, founder of IDEO, TED Talks section, TED.com, filmed March 2012, www.ted.com/talks/david_kelley_how_to_build_your_creative_confidence?language=en

Lynda.com (Online video tutorials to help you learn software, creative, and business skills), www.lynda.com

The Viral Video Manifesto: Why Everything You Know Is Wrong and How to Do What Really Works, by Stephen Voltz and Fritz Grobe (McGraw-Hill, 2012)

• INTERVIEW QUESTIONS •

How would you define creativity?

What would you recommend that an organization could do to develop a culture of creativity?

How can you get people to reenvision their environment so that they see the extraordinary in it?

How do you get people to talk and think about creativity?

Are there tools that you would recommend to a library if it is trying to develop a culture of creativity? Books to recommend?

What mind-sets, qualities, or talents have you found to characterize creative people whom you admire and how would you cultivate these attributes in a staff?

What would you look for if you were trying to hire people who "think differently"?

What do you think are the biggest barriers to creativity in an organization and how might they be addressed?

You talk about "using your brand in a nontraditional way to show your personality." What do you think that might look like at a public library?

What is the most important thing that you have learned about creativity and organizations?

What do you think the leaders of organizations need to do if they want to encourage a culture of creativity?

If you had ten minutes to talk with library directors about today's libraries, what would you tell them to do differently to be unforgettable or to communicate in an unforgettable way with their communities?

5

ADVOCATES FOR THE CREATORS

MARGOT ATWELL
Kickstarter

• WHY THIS TOPIC •

I support the idea of libraries being advocates for the arts and collaborators with artists. A partnership has always existed between libraries and the arts, and it only makes sense to explore how to sustain and expand this mutually beneficial relationship. In addition, libraries are ideally suited to support and mentor local creators such as writers, artists, and musicians and have a built-in audience with whom to share the works of those creators. The challenge is to define *how* libraries can be creative advocates. If you are interested in reading more about this topic, visit the website of the Library as Incubator Project (www.library asincubatorproject.org), a project started by graduate students getting their master's degrees in library science. The website has some wonderful examples about how libraries can become incubators for the arts. This was my starting point for learning about this concept and what led me to explore it further as a topic for this book.

• WHY THIS ORGANIZATION •

Kickstarter is the granddaddy of crowdfunding organizations. Crowdfunding is the process of raising many small donations from a large number of people to support a project, generally via use of the Internet. Kickstarter was established specifically to fund creative projects, and its mission is to bring creative projects to life. Since Kickstarter was launched in 2009, 6.7 million people have pledged one billion dollars, funding 66,000 creative projects. Kickstarter was of interest to me because, as a business, its entire reason for being is to support creative endeavors. My hope was to identify from the company's perspective new ways that libraries might do more to assist and promote creators at the local community level.

I talked with Margot Atwell at Kickstarter. Margot came out of the publishing world, is a library lover, and was a very creative thinker about the questions I asked. We discussed how libraries are using Kickstarter, how they might use Kickstarter in the future, and what libraries can learn from how Kickstarter supports the development of creative projects at libraries.

• INSIGHTS FROM THIS INTERVIEW •

LEARNING

Conveying the passion of a creator is core to building a community of support. Passion was a word that came up over and over in my discussion with Margot. Kickstarter has been extraordinarily successful in finding supporters for so many thousands of projects partially because it does everything possible to help creators convey their energy and enthusiasm for their projects. This in turn is one of the most important tools to drive interest and support. There are thousands of intriguing ideas on Kickstarter, but the most successful ones are those which successfully communicate the delight and enthusiasm the creators have for their projects. It is clear that the more people can tap the emotional energy being conveyed by a project creator, the more interested and vested they are in the project concept.

Kickstarter has discovered a very simple truth. The company advises creators to be open, honest, and, above all, themselves. As a result, what is conveyed by Kickstarter projects is the creators' desire to generate something new and their enthusiasm about doing that. Looking at Kickstarter projects is just plain interesting, and many people visit the website out of curiosity and not because they are planning to contribute funds to a project. This tells you a lot about the energy that goes into the projects.

Each creator on Kickstarter must make a video about his or her project. As part of this video, the creator talks about why he or she is so energized at the idea of being able to create the featured product/service. The video allows the creator to talk directly to the people who might fund the project. The video becomes the tool that allows a creator to have a conversation with potential funders. And, even in today's technologically driven world, a personal conversation is still the most effective way to communicate.

▶ Implication

Libraries must learn to convey their passion for what they do if they want to engage the attention of a broader audience. Libraries are very good at sharing information, teaching, and educating. Once people walk through the door of a library, they come back because they discover the riches that the library provides. However, libraries struggle to get people to walk into the library the first time. Why? People are intimidated by all of those books and smart people in one place; or they still think that a library is a warehouse for books where stern librarians shush visitors, which just does not seem like a place they want to spend time; or they think that a library provides only books for borrowing and they want to read on a Kindle. The common denominator in all of these views of the library is a lack of knowledge about what today's library really is. When people think this way, it means that either we have not reached those people with the story about today's library or we have reached them but the story did not have enough impact to register with the listeners.

My bet is that people hear our story but it does not register because it is not powerful and emotional. Librarians are good at telling our stories in a factual, accurate, and detailed way—we have been trained to be all of those things—but if you get us in a conversation about what we do, we suddenly become passionate. What we do matters! We have the passion, but now we need to learn to show it to the world.

▶ Ideas

Ask all staff members at your library to identify one thing they do at the library that they love and that absolutely makes their day when they get to do it. Then, ask for volunteers to do a very short video (thirty seconds max) about the part of the job that they love. The only thing they have to do in the video is make sure they convey their enthusiasm. Ask the participants in this process to vote and identify the three best videos (meaning the ones which most accurately convey the speakers' energy and enthusiasm), and then share those videos online with library patrons. If emotional engagement is something that we want to include in our marketing and communications, we need to begin by experimenting with this idea and learning what does and does not work in terms of creating a powerful connection with the viewer.

Another way to approach this might be to identify one of the drier, less exciting resources offered by the library and create a contest out of promoting that resource. Whoever can create a video about one boring resource that gets *x* number of "likes" on Facebook first wins. The goal initially is not to get Facebook likes but to get staff engaged with the idea of creating videos that capture attention regardless of the topic.

Have the people doing programs at your library promote the programs themselves using a very short video. The people who do programs at your library most likely have tremendous energy and passion for what they are doing. By taking a video of the presenter, you provide him or her with an opportunity to talk directly to potential audience members about the program. Think about how much more powerful this could be as a way to build interest in a program than pictures on a flyer or words in a newsletter (although these can also be very useful and certainly should not be eliminated from your promotional efforts). This idea could be extended to any or all of the social media channels that your library uses.

LEARNING

Connecting people on a human level creates powerful bonds. Creators at Kickstarter use video to convey their energy and passion for their work. However, they also use video to talk about who they are as individuals and their stories. This makes a real difference to the people who want to fund their projects. If you feel a human connection with someone because you know how that person thinks, what his or her life story is, and how he or she is going to approach his or her work, you are going to be much more likely to want to support what that person is doing.

Kickstarter provides additional opportunities for creators to convey information about themselves by encouraging them to do regular project updates with their funders. Project updates create back-and-forth conversations that help build the relationships between creators and funders. When a creator does a second or third (or more!) project, he or she frequently goes back to his or her original funders to obtain their involvement in these subsequent projects. This makes a lot of sense from the perspective that the better you know someone, the more likely you are going to give that person money and support.

▶ Implication

The likelihood of a community being supportive of the local library will increase if the community knows the library staff on a personal level and understands why these people care so passionately about the library. Librarians have always taken great pride in providing accurate, detailed, and nonbiased information and services. In addition, many are very good at building professional relationships with the community members who use the library. The more often that community members get to know librarians as individuals, and understand their passion and dedication, the more often those community members will stand up to support the library when it is time to establish budgets.

However, as the world has become more complicated and sometimes dangerous, some public librarians have felt the need to protect themselves by reducing the amount that the public knows about them, assuming that this will make them less of a target for problematic individuals. I understand this concern. No one wants to find someone following him or her out to the parking lot at night. However, my viewpoint is that you can connect on a human level without putting yourself in harm's way by applying basic common sense. You can avoid sharing too much by sharing only the parts of you that are relevant to the library but not your personal life.

▶ Ideas

Be open to connecting with library users on a human level. A simple example of this is wearing name tags while we work at public service desks so people feel like they are talking to real people versus nameless "staff" persons. I believe strongly that my name tag should have both my first and last names on it, and I would like all of my staff to do the same because to me it is professional. However, I will settle for a first name only if a staff member believes having both names is problematic. Another way of developing connections would be to set up a bulletin board with pictures of the library staff members and their names as a way of helping the public figure out with whom they are interacting. A library could also include monthly articles about library staff in its newsletter. All of these ideas can be done without making any staff members more vulnerable while still informing the public about the people who are available to help them at the library.

Share information that makes the public see the library and the librarians in a real way. For example, include an article in your library newsletter (or on your website) that highlights some of the things librarians do when they are outside the library, such as singing in a local chorus or knitting hats for new babies at the local hospital. You could post a short video online about what happens at the library before the doors open or include a behind-the-scenes video of the librarians' work area or staff room. Do not script these videos; just shoot them and share them. The goal is to make your library users feel like they know the people who work at the library on a very real, human level.

Get out of the library into the community so more people can get to know you. There are multiple ways library employees might do this. Librarians can teach classes out in the community, go to the local farmers market and sign folks up for library cards, or hold a story time at the local park instead of in the library. If you provide library cards to local community college students, it might be more effective to go to the college campus, sit in the main gathering area and talk to students versus waiting for them to come to the library. If your community has special events, like Fourth of July or Halloween parades, make sure the library participates in them. The more people see librarians outside of the library, the more they are going to see us as individuals versus anonymous librarians.

Be yourself when you are representing the library. I always say that as a library director, I have no shame. To support the library and put a real face on the library for the community, I have kissed a pig, scooped ice cream, and told silly stories about myself to large community groups. My goal is to change the stereotype of the library director as a serious person who does not laugh much and probably is not much fun to hang out around. I want people to see me (and by association Curtis Memorial Library) as an interesting, different, slightly irreverent person whom they would enjoy getting to know. I want everyone in my community to feel like they know me personally even if they do not because it will make them feel much more comfortable about walking into Curtis Library. No, I do not worry about looking and acting like a professional. I know that I am a professional and that I am very good at my job. I do not have to convince people of this by wearing a business suit and carrying a briefcase. Rather, I want to convince them that I am a real, interesting person who, by association, makes the library a real, interesting place.

LEARNING

Storytelling can help build a groundswell of interest in an idea. Essentially, everything that Kickstarter does is a form of storytelling. Instead of asking creators to provide bullet points in a PowerPoint presentation to sell their ideas to possible supporters, Kickstarter asks creators to develop videos in which they talk about their ideas from their personal viewpoints, conveying their passion and enthusiasm directly to the possible funders. By asking creators to talk about themselves and their lives, Kickstarter casts them in the role of hero or protagonist in their own stories. By making a Kickstarter campaign an all-or-nothing opportunity, the company creates tension and energy around creators' projects that contributors can help resolve by providing funding. All of these factors help turn Kickstarter projects into stories versus business proposals. And because storytelling evokes emotions in the listeners, this is a powerful way to engage and captivate the listeners. In fact, the projects that are most successful at Kickstarter include a strong element of storytelling in the information provided to potential funders.

▶ Implication

Librarians can build more support and involvement for what we do if we start to tell more stories and create fewer PowerPoint presentations. Yes, librarians are accurate and factual. However, most of us joined this profession also because we love stories and reading and dreams and ideas and we are all creative (see the previous chapter on creativity). As a profession, we could be much more powerful if we started telling more stories and conveyed less factual information. I am probably one of the worst offenders when it comes to this. I came out of the business world, and bullet points are my default. I love them because they force you to be concise and specific, but they can also make you very boring. So, my personal challenge over the past few years has been to try to use almost no words on my PowerPoint presentations when I get up in front of an audience. Instead, I use pictures and I talk about those pictures. This has definitely improved my ability to capture and hold the attention of an audience, but I do still use the PowerPoint presentation as a crutch. My next goal is to take this process one step further. I want to be able to do my own personal TED talk when I do presentations. This means that I will need to get rid of my reliance on PowerPoint and just tell a story. If I can do this, capture and hold my audience's attention (as a storyteller), then I guarantee that people will walk away remembering and having taken to heart what I had to say.

Learning to be good storytellers is a huge opportunity for the library profession. Storytelling is a powerful tool because it conveys both information and emotion. People will remember what they hear when it is connected to an emotion. Storytelling can be used as part of library advocacy, outreach, marketing, teaching, or any other event that puts library employees in front of the public. Author Maya Angelou expressed this beautifully when she said, "I've learned that people will forget what you said, people will forget what you did, but people will never forget how you made them feel." Stories are also a wonderful tool because they allow you to turn complex ideas into simple stories that grab the listeners' emotions and allow them to understand quickly what you are saying.

▶ Ideas

Include storytelling in staff training. Every member of a library's staff should at least understand what storytelling is, even if they do not feel comfortable doing it themselves. By knowing what is involved in storytelling, they can be more supportive of the staff members who do engage in it. Including storytelling in official training also makes clear that it is a valued skill in the work of the library. At staff meetings, discuss storytelling—what storytelling is, what a great storyteller does, how storytelling might be used by librarians. Then, as appropriate, ask staff members at a staff meeting to volunteer to "tell a story" about something for which they have responsibility versus giving a report. Talk about how it felt to hear a story. Was it more or less compelling than listening to a report? Identify how storytelling might be used more in interactions with the public. Ask library staff members to watch how the children's librarians do their story time programs. A good children's librarian is a natural storyteller, and you can learn a great deal about good storytelling just by watching what they do.

Try doing a presentation with no PowerPoint slides and just focus on telling a story. Do this in a no-risk situation first, such as at a staff meeting. Tell your audience what you are doing and ask for their feedback when you are done. Then, take your show on the road and do a storytelling session in a public environment, such as when you do a program about how to use Kickstarter. You do not have to eliminate backup data but have it available at the end of a presentation instead. *Note:* Sometimes due to the nature of the audience for your presentation or what you are presenting, you must use PowerPoint slides. This is okay. The goal of this idea is not to eliminate completely the use of PowerPoint in your work process. Rather, it is to provide you with another tool (storytelling) that can be extraordinarily powerful in the right situation.

LEARNING

Video is a powerful tool that can vividly convey authenticity. Video is a key tool used by every Kickstarter project creator to explain what he or she is doing and to tell his or her story. The company's statistics of use (6.7 million people have pledged over one billion dollars in support for projects on Kickstarter) demonstrate what a powerful tool video has been in telling stories in a persuasive way that drives support. This is not to say that the videos produced by Kickstarter creators are all high quality with great production values. In fact, many of them are amateurish with terrible production values. However, what they have in common is the ability to share the story of a project creator in a direct, immediate way that gets your attention.

▶ Implication

Libraries could be using video much more as a tool to develop awareness, support, and involvement. The ability of video to develop a conversation between the person who produces it and the person who watches it makes it an obvious tool of value for libraries that are always trying to find better ways of connecting with their communities. However, librarians do not seem to have figured out how to do videos effectively. I do not get excited by many of the library-produced videos that I see because most librarians still use videos as a tool to educate versus as a tool to connect. If we can start using videos more to "talk with" our library's users, then there is potential in this tool to vastly expand our audience.

▶ Ideas

Write a grant or find a donor to fund the purchase of video cameras or cell phones with video capacity for your service desks. Make taking videos part of every person's job at the library. Develop a video bank where, at the end of each day, videos can be downloaded and shared with the entire staff. As part of downloading a video, staff members could share ideas about how a specific video might be used. The idea is that taking and using videos becomes part of your library's culture versus something you do only on special occasions. I like the idea of making this part of everyone's job because I think that will expand the scope of the videos that are shot. If you make it the responsibility of one individual, you will be limited by how much that one person can do. If you ask many employees to take videos, it becomes more likely that someone will have a camera in hand when the opportunity to capture the thoughts, ideas, and emotions of library users presents itself.

Ask staff members to be on the lookout for highly effective videos and to share them with the rest of the library's employees. Create a location online where employees can post the videos and comment about what they think makes the videos powerful. The goal of this idea is to raise awareness as to the power in videos and to help employees start evaluating why a video does or does not work.

LEARNING

Many people are willing to support good ideas with funding, but to get their support, you need to do your homework. Kickstarter's great story is that over 68,000 projects have been successfully funded by 6,865,444 funders. There are people everywhere who are fascinated by new ideas and love to support their development. However, on the other side of the equation, over 95,000 projects have not reached the goal of 100 percent funding support and so were unsuccessful. To reach people and get their support on Kickstarter, you need to do the work to get their attention. Kickstarter provides a "Creator Handbook" that describes what you have to do to be successful and includes a lot of very helpful information (www.kickstarter.com/help/hand book). Yet, there are still projects that do not get funded. Why? Sometimes it is just because an idea is not very good. However, it is often because project creators do not do the work necessary to get support. They may not do a good job of telling their story with passion and enthusiasm, or they do not "rally the troops" (meaning family and friends) to provide the initial support that gets the project off the ground, or they do not create a video to support their storytelling. Bottom line: the creators did not do the work to make the project happen.

▶ Implication

If you are not getting the support that you want for your library, possibly you are not doing the work to make it happen. The day of libraries automatically getting support and funding are gone. Libraries need to create positive, compelling reasons as to why their communities should continue to fund them. As librarians and library leaders, every day we must put time and energy into making this happen because no one will fund our libraries without a good reason for doing so, no matter how big or how small the libraries are. If you are struggling with funding, then you need to (a) go through all of the ways that you can build support and make sure you are doing them and/or (b) find a better, more convincing way to persuade people that supporting your library will benefit them.

▶ Idea

Before you start developing your next budget, set up a conversation with the person in your community who is most vocal about why the library should not be supported financially. (This idea is hard to do, but it can work!) You know who those people are. Every year you hear from them, in one way or another, about why they do not want to pay for the library with their tax dollars. Find someone who knows them and see if that person will facilitate a chat, or directly invite them to the library for a cup of coffee. Prepare for these meetings like they are meetings with the president of the United States. Be able to speak clearly and compellingly about the library and what it does for your community. Have your facts in hand about measures of use and funding. Have a short story about how the library has made a difference in the life of someone in your community. When you meet with people who do not support your library, give them everything you have got in terms of information and passion. Then, after you are finished, stop and listen. Hear what they have to say. Ask questions but do not argue. Listen. Then listen some more. Do they have a real issue or do they just not have enough information (which you can give them)? If you go through this process, I can guarantee you that at least some of the folks you meet with will change their attitudes. Why? You have done the work to present a compelling argument; they have heard the argument and are willing to change their perspective. And if worse comes to worst and their attitude does not change at all, you will have gained a lot of valuable insight into what their concerns are and whether you can address them.

LEARNING

Once a creator develops relationships with funders, he or she can tap those sources for future support. Funders who participate in Kickstarter get regular updates about the projects at hand from the creators. When starting a new project, a creator may go back to his or her original funders to get support. The likelihood is high that they will support new projects because he or she has already developed relationships with them.

▶ Implication

The act of donating to support an enterprise creates a bond that may be tapped more than once. When people give money through Kickstarter, they are making a statement that they believe in what the creators are trying to do. This is a powerful declaration, one that can create a strong sense of relationship between creators and funders that can be tapped for future ideas, information, and financial support. Libraries develop similar relationships when they do fund-raising. Donors are indicating their support for the library's role in the community. When the library develops new programs, this is the most obvious group to start with in terms of fund-raising because, as donors, they have already indicated that they believe in the library's mission.

▶ Idea

Facilitate the establishment of connections among different groups in the community. The library can do this because it is a trusted resource. At Curtis Library, we developed an online forum, called Curtis Creative Spaces (www.curtiscreativespaces.com), for local creators, meaning artists, crafters, writers, and musicians. It is free for the creators, and our goal is simply to provide a larger audience for local creators than what they might get initially on their own. Each month we feature a different creator. To increase awareness for the website, we have raffled off small pieces of art by the featured creators. To participate, people need only visit the website and share their contact information. This endeavor has been very successful, and we have built up a good list of e-mail contacts of people interested in the site. However, after I talked to Margot at Kickstarter, I realized that we had missed an opportunity by not sharing the names of people interested in the raffles with the artists whose works were raffled off. If we had done that, the artists could have made contact with the people (obviously in a nonintrusive way) to let them know how they can learn more about their art. Obviously, you have to be careful to protect people's privacy and not infringe on their good nature, but you also should be aware of when you can help make connections in the community.

LEARNING

Rewarding people for participating in a project is a viable way of developing community support. Every Kickstarter project has to include rewards to funders. The rewards can take almost any form, but generally they are related to the project being funded. While rewards do not make or break a project, creative rewards can help build a groundswell of support for a project. By providing rewards that incorporate some component of the project, creators are giving funders the opportunity to participate actively in the project and to become part of the project community and the project experience. Thus, rewards do play an important role in developing a groundswell of interest and, ultimately, support.

▶ Implication

Rewards can be useful tools to build awareness of and a sense of community for library projects. The use of rewards by libraries is sometimes seen as a form of bribery to get people to participate in an activity, or it is perceived as a form of payment, again, to get people to participate. However, used in the Kickstarter way, rewards are really a form of marketing that can build awareness about and support for a project as well as create a sense of participation and "specialness" for being part of a project in the capacity of funder. There is nothing intrinsically wrong with using rewards in a nonprofit setting as long as the end result of providing the rewards somehow supports and furthers the purpose of the organization and does not benefit any one person or group financially.

▶ Idea

Experiment with using rewards to build awareness about events and programs. For example, at Curtis Library, as mentioned earlier, we built a website dedicated to promoting the art, music, and writing of local creators. To draw attention to the website and convince people to check it out, we held a raffle for a free piece of art by one of the people featured on the site. To participate, all people had to do was visit the website and register. The first time we tried this, we were very low key about it because we did not want people to feel like we were bribing them to go to the website. The second time we tried it, we said to heck with that—we are not bribing folks, we are providing them with a great opportunity to learn about artists in our community, and we are going to promote this reward! That approach worked, and we had many community members participate in the raffle and then send e-mails with positive input about both the raffle and the website. Now we do not think of rewards as bribing people but rather as giving them an incentive to discover something that we are pretty darn sure they will love.

LEARNING

Asking the people who are responsible for a project to participate in developing support for that project is an important and appropriate methodology for creating a groundswell of interest. I learned that many projects at Kickstarter did not reach the mandatory goal of 100 percent funding. When I asked why, the response was that many people did not understand that they could not just post an idea and expect the money to come flying in the door. The creator has a responsibility to get things off the ground by initiating interest and participation. No one wants to be part of a "loser" project, so it is important to get funders and money as quickly as possible. The way to create a tsunami of support is for each creator to tap his or her personal network, rounding up family and friends to participate in funding the project. Once there is initial support on the books, potential funders are much more likely to jump on the bandwagon.

▶ Implication

Creating participation and interest in a program or project at the library requires that both the library and the presenter promote the event. It is only logical that the more people who promote an event or program at the library, the more likely that people will hear about it and check it out. Beyond that, word-of-mouth support from a friend or someone you know is probably the most effective way of promoting and supporting an event at the library. No one should be able to opt out of this responsibility, particularly not those who are putting on the program. Sometimes presenters like to avoid this responsibility because they see their only job as doing the presentation. They want someone else to publicize what they are doing. Asking a presenter to participate in the process of marketing his or her program means that the presenter must make an effort to get people to attend, and invariably, the resulting turnout is better than it would have been without the presenter's involvement.

▶ Idea

Ask anyone who is presenting at the library to take responsibility for a specific part of promoting the event. Libraries are constantly providing programs and training and special events for the public. Often the people who do these events expect the library employees to do all of the work to promote the event to the public. If I am paying someone to do a program, I do not mind promoting it. However, if someone requests to do a program at the library, I think it is perfectly appropriate to ask that individual to take ownership for promoting the event. Library employees have limited capacity to develop and distribute marketing, and getting presenters involved frees up the staff from this work and ensures that the presenters care about the success of their programs.

LEARNING

Organizations that can connect two very different groups in a shared purpose have great value. Kickstarter gives creators the tools to develop the stories of their projects and then share those stories with enough people so that those who are interested in the stories and want to help determine how they end can sign up. In this process, Kickstarter becomes the bridge between these two very different groups of people—creators and funders. Having an organization like Kickstarter as the go-between or connector between creators and funders is obviously valued, given the huge success of Kickstarter.

▶ Implication

Libraries are one of the most vital, active connectors in our society's communities. We need to promote this role. People want and value connections. Everyone needs an informal network of touch points to run their lives. People will support organizations that help them make those connections. However, people need to understand how the organization helps them in making those connections. At Kickstarter, this is obvious. At the local library, the role of the library in building connections across the community is less obvious, so the library needs to do more to communicate how it does this.

▶ Ideas

Use your library's newsletter or website to promote how the library builds connections. When you are promoting events, talk about the ways those events will create their own small communities of connections. Tell stories. Help your community understand what it means when you tell them the library builds community. At Curtis Library, we have a small group of individuals who attend a craft meet-up every week. They bring whatever project they are working on at the time and sit and chat while they work. They have become great friends and found this is a wonderful way of connecting with others in the community who share a similar passion. We did an article in a library newsletter about one of the participants. She told the story about how she has found friends and a place to belong in this group. When I tell others in the community this story, they immediately understand how the library facilitated those connections and why that matters. But if you do not tell the stories, people will not always understand how the library does this work and why they should support it.

Be willing to have the library try new ways of connecting people. Curtis Library never provided connections between creators and the community in the past, yet it was an obvious way that we could support the creation of local content in our community while still working within the library's traditional footprint. As libraries consider what roles they can appropriately take on for their communities, it makes sense to look carefully at ways that they can continue to be connecters and not to be afraid of roles that seem very different from the past. Connecting the community with local creators is one example. How about providing a location in the library for genealogists to connect with one another or some space for use as a business incubator where people starting small businesses can share ideas and help motivate one another to success? These are different from the library's traditional role in the past, yet at the same time they are examples of what the library has done from its inception—connect people.

• THE BIG IDEAS FROM THIS INTERVIEW •

I loved talking to Margot about Kickstarter. Even though she came out of a very traditional industry (publishing), she is open to new ideas and new ways of thinking and, as such, was the perfect person to talk with about what libraries can learn from the rest of the world.

I think the first learning, "Conveying the passion of a creator is core to building a community of support," is an idea with huge potential to change how libraries operate. If libraries are not garnering the support in their communities that they think they should have, the issue may be that librarians need to find new ways of communicating what libraries do that is so important.

Connected to this is the learning that "Storytelling can help build a groundswell of interest in an idea." Librarians live in a world created and populated by storytellers, yet we are not very good at telling stories ourselves. Stories can be such important tools in building support that librarians need to become experts at storytelling.

I also think that the last learning, "Organizations that can connect two very different groups in a shared purpose have great value," is important because it speaks directly to the value of being a connector, which is something that all libraries do already, whether they talk about it or not. If we live in a time when connections are ever more important, then communicating the fact that libraries are expert at helping people make connections will play an important role in increasing their value for their communities.

• SUMMARY OF WHAT I LEARNED •

- Conveying the passion of a creator is core to building a community of support.
- Connecting people on a human level creates powerful bonds.
- Storytelling can help build a groundswell of interest in an idea.
- Video is a powerful tool that can vividly convey authenticity.
- Many people are willing to support good ideas with funding, but to get their support, you need to do your homework.
- Once a creator develops relationships with funders, he or she can tap those sources for future support.

- Rewarding people for participating in a project is a viable way of developing community support.
- Asking the people who are responsible for a project to participate in developing support for that project is an important and appropriate methodology for creating a groundswell of interest.
- Organizations that can connect two very different groups in a shared purpose have great value.

• RESOURCES •

Kickstarter.com (Bring your creative project to life), www. kickstarter.com

The Library as Incubator Project, www. libraryasincubatorproject.org

The Story Factor: Inspiration, Influence, and Persuasion through the Art of Storytelling, by Annette Simmons (Basic Books, 2009)

• INTERVIEW QUESTIONS •

What do you think attracts a community of people to support a creative project? The fact that there is a clear beginning and end to the project? The fact that rewards are offered? Just a cool idea?

It seems that the story is as important as the product/service on Kickstarter in developing interest in a project. Do you have thoughts about that?

When you read Kickstarter project ideas, you often end up feeling like you know the person who "owns" the project. Do you think this sense of a personal connection helps build interest in a project?

What do you think libraries can learn from Kickstarter in terms of supporting the local creative environment?

Libraries frequently provide new services to their communities (like free e-books), but they do not do a great job of marketing those services or building awareness about them. What could libraries learn from Kickstarter projects that are successful in terms of "selling" their idea?

What do you think are the most effective ways that libraries have successfully used Kickstarter to support creativity in their communities?

It seems like there is a *lot* of information online (consultants) for people interested in how to do a Kickstarter project. What if libraries provided classes about how to do a successful project on Kickstarter and then had preliminary "judging" before the project went to Kickstarter to (a) hone the idea and (b) build interest in and awareness of the idea at a very local level? Good idea or bad?

I think a lot of people who participate in backing projects get subsequently inspired to do creative work themselves. Does Kickstarter know the percentage of its projects that come from people who were previously inspired by other Kickstarter projects?

CUSTOMER SERVICE

CHRIS WILSON

L.L.Bean

• WHY THIS TOPIC •

What is great customer service? If you ask that question in a library, you are likely to get many different responses. To some library employees, it is "delighting the customer." To others, it is "treating everyone the same." To still others, it is providing services efficiently and effectively or simply the process of smiling and being pleasant to library users. It is unlikely that you will find one consistent answer in one library, much less in the profession as a whole.

How do libraries train employees to deliver great customer service? My experience has been that many libraries initiate sporadic customer service training when a problem with customer service happens. A library user complains because someone at the circulation desk was rude to him or her—time for customer service training! The result of this approach is that customer service training becomes something to dread because it means the library staff did something wrong and now they have to learn the right way. Employees approach the training feeling defensive, and who can blame them?

I would far rather see customer service discussions, education, and awareness become part of the daily life of the library. If libraries truly want to transform themselves, they need to understand how to make the customer the center of their universe. Customer service needs to be part of a library's values statement. It needs to be discussed every day among library employees. To help in this process, this chapter focuses on a business that lives customer service, day in and day out, as part of its organizational DNA to get a better understanding of how libraries might do the same.

• WHY THIS ORGANIZATION •

L.L.Bean has been in business since 1912, and its guiding value has always been customer service. The golden rule of the company's founder, Leon L. Bean, was "Sell good merchandise at a reasonable profit, treat your customers like human beings, and they will always come back for more." This is still the company's driving value today. Anyone who has spent any time interacting with L.L.Bean figures out very quickly that its goal is to do right by the customer, regardless of whether the interaction takes place in one of their retail stores, online, or via the telephone. The company guarantees 100 percent satisfaction with its products, and they mean it. Anyone who lives in Maine has stories about a piece of clothing or luggage or outdoor gear that they hesitantly took back to L.L.Bean because it had some small flaw. Universally, the company's response is to replace these things immediately, with no questions asked and no hassle. Anyone who has this experience is startled the first time it happens because they do not have to justify bringing the product back, they get no argument from L.L.Bean employees, and any problems are resolved quickly. This just goes to show how unusual this type of customer experience is in today's retail world.

L.L.Bean is a Maine company, and they are very supportive of local individuals and organizations and were kind enough to set up an interview for me with Chris Wilson, Senior Vice President of Direct Channel at L.L.Bean. We had a great discussion about how L.L.Bean thinks about its customers, and he gave me a peek at some of the ways that the company delivers its world-class customer service.

• INSIGHTS FROM THIS INTERVIEW •

LEARNING

In an organization that is committed to being customer-centric, clear and concise communication ensures that everyone understands what this means. At L.L.Bean, there is no confusion about customer service. Every person who works there can tell you the guiding principle of customer service as exemplified by the company's determination to provide 100 percent customer satisfaction. Every new employee who starts at L.L.Bean learns about the founder's goal of "treating your customers like human beings," and everyone who works in the company understands what that means. During our interview, Chris indicated that there is not a lot of debate at L.L.Bean when new projects happen around customer service. The focus is consistently on doing the right thing for the customer, and if there is a cost attached to this, then that cost is paid. It struck me when I talked to Chris that customer service is so embedded in the company's culture that no one even considers any other perspective. Customer service is the guiding light for the company, and no other values even come close to it in terms of importance.

▶ Implication

One concise definition of customer service that everyone understands can help hardwire the concept into an organization. When you talk to any L.L.Bean employee, it is clear that each understands what customer service means to the organization and what it means to his or her work. This understanding is the same whether you are talking to someone who works in the warehouse only at Christmastime or the senior vice president of marketing. The company's guiding principle about customer service that employees hear is always the same (100 percent satisfaction guarantee), and they understand that they will receive full support in achieving that goal. The consistency and regular repetition of the guiding principle ensure that there is no confusion about customer service, ever.

▶ Idea

Develop a customer service principle or motto for your library. Libraries do not
have a nice motto about customer service, articulated by their founder,
to define the path to customer satisfaction. But why not develop one?
Ask your community members what good customer service means to
them. The odds are good that they will say something along these
lines: "Good customer service means that you really listened to what I
had to say, you addressed my question(s) quickly, you were nice to me,
and you did not make me go to six people to get what I wanted in the
library." Take what they say and turn it into your own customer service
principle. In the process, make sure that you do not make your principle any longer or more complicated than L.L.Bean's guideline
(which is only twenty-one words long). Ask all library employees to
talk about the customer service motto and hash it through until they
are sure they understand it front to back and back to front. Then,
repeat that motto everywhere and to everyone. When someone is confused about what to do in a customer service situation, pull out the
motto to see if it answers the person's question; it should. The key
point is to develop one communication about customer service that
is simple to understand and easy to remember. Then, hold everyone
(employees, the library director, the library board) accountable to
remember the principle and put it to work.

LEARNING

*In a truly customer-centric organization, the first question asked in all situa-
tions becomes "What is the right thing to do for the customer?"* There is no
question that at L.L.Bean the customer's needs are primary even
when this is not always beneficial to the organization. The company's 100 percent satisfaction guarantee is a great example of this.
The promise is that the company's merchandise will hold up and
satisfy you—period. No "but" or qualifications are part of the statement. You can have an L.L.Bean product for ten years, but if something breaks, you can take it back to the store and they will replace
it with no questions asked. Obviously, this does not benefit the company financially. However, for this organization, it is the definition

of what being customer-centric means, and it has truly become the primary guideline for how the business operates.

▶ Implication

If an organization is truly customer-centric, that perspective should permeate every aspect of how it operates. If being customer-centric is important to a library, then that concept will be part of every aspect of how the library operates. All library employees will understand how their jobs affect the customers, whether they have direct interaction with them or not. Strategic planning will incorporate a discussion about customer service and its role in helping the library achieve its objectives. Employees will talk about customer service regularly, and the default approach to answering any questions about how to manage the library will be "What is right for library users?" Instead of initiating a work process because it makes life easier for library staff, libraries will put in place work processes that improve the customers' experience in the library. Customer satisfaction will go from being something discussed once every six months or when there is a problem to being the everyday, all-the-time, guiding light for the library.

▶ Ideas

Develop a statement for every job description at your library that articulates (a) who the customer (internal or external) is for that job and (b) what customer service looks like for that job. Some jobs at a library are "customer facing" and some are internally oriented. However, every job has a customer whose needs should be met, whether that customer is internal or external. Defining who the customer is for a job and the expectations for how that customer's needs are met will begin the process of embedding a customer service orientation into every job in the library. Also, including customer service as part of every job description establishes a link between compensation and customer service that will further embed it as part of the culture.

Do an audit of your library's strategic planning documents (values, mission, and vision statements) to understand the degree to which customer satisfaction drives the organization. This is a simple but revealing activity. Go through your library's strategic documents and identify how often and in what capacity customer service is mentioned as part of your library's strategic direction. Customer service cannot just be assumed to be important. It needs to be part of the articulated values of the library to ensure that everyone is marching in the same direction. If it is missing from these documents, this is a good indication that it is time to revisit the library's strategic priorities. I will not tell a lie: as I started writing this book, I did an audit of the strategic documents at my own library and realized (with some degree of embarrassment) that customer service was not identified as one of the guiding values at Curtis Memorial Library. I know that the library staff work hard to provide great customer service, and generally our library users are very happy with it. However, could we take it to a whole new level of excellence by writing in customer service as one of our guiding values? I do not know the answer, but I can tell you that, in the near future, we will definitely be updating the Curtis Library values statement to include it.

LEARNING

The process of knowing your customers and understanding what they want from your business never stops. Defining who the L.L.Bean customers are and then understanding what they want from the company seems to be a nonstop activity at the company. L.L.Bean engages in a regular conversation with its customers in a variety of ways. If you purchase anything from L.L.Bean (over the phone, via the website, or in the store), you are automatically eligible for a weekly satisfaction survey. There are also opportunities for customers to provide feedback about any aspect of their L.L.Bean experience via e-mail and phone. The company does brand-level surveys, and it does blind studies in which L.L.Bean is only one of multiple companies asking for consumer feedback. The company is also now in the process of developing computer programs to help them quickly review and mine open-ended comments for information. This is only a short list of the many forms of customer interaction that takes place at L.L.Bean.

What does L.L.Bean do with this huge amount of information flowing into the organization? One of the more intriguing concepts mentioned is something the company calls a "journey map." Essentially, a journey map identifies a customer type, such as a mom with kids who is buying items to get the kids ready for school. L.L.Bean will develop scenarios of the entire process that the mom goes through to interact with and purchase products from the company. Among the things considered are how the mom learned about L.L.Bean, how she looked for an item (online, in a catalog, in the store), how she decided if that was the right item, and how she purchased the item. The mom's entire interaction with L.L.Bean is mapped out and all of the potential touch points between the mom and the company are identified. Then, the company figures out what it can do to quickly and easily get that mom from the beginning of the purchase process to the end point in as smooth and frictionless a way as possible. Bottom line: the company collects lots and lots of information about its customers with the goal of using that information to simplify and streamline the customers' interactions with the company and make their experience as positive as possible.

► Implication

Libraries have the opportunity to learn a great deal about their customers beyond basic demographics and to use that information to provide a better customer experience in the library. Imagine if libraries created journey maps for their customers, similar to what L.L.Bean does, thinking about all of the ways that customers touch the library and how we might improve those interactions. I know that frequently libraries bring out the issue of customer privacy as a reason for not collecting more information about customers. However, if librarians allow our patrons to opt in or opt out of sharing information and if we aggregate information into similar groups of people (thereby eliminating any possibility of identifying individuals), then we could easily address privacy concerns. And the benefits from thinking more about our customers and doing more to understand what they want from our libraries would be immense.

If you are interested in the concept of developing a journey map, check out the article "Using Customer Journey Maps to Improve Customer Experience," by Adam Richardson, in the *Harvard Business Review* (https://blogs.hbr.org/2010/11/using-customer-journey-maps-to). Richards provides information about journey maps and how they can be used as well providing a template that can be adapted for use by libraries. He also defines the process that customers go through to purchase a product:

- Develop awareness about the product/service
- Research information about it
- Purchase the product
- Take the product home and use it (called the OOBE, or out-of-box experience)

The journey map identifies for each of these stages the actions taken by the customer, his or her motivations, the questions the customer may have, and the barriers that may keep him or her from moving on to the next step. By understanding the particular questions and barriers to movement, an organization can develop processes to eliminate questions or barriers or find ways to walk customers through barriers quickly and easily.

▶ Ideas

Test one simple way to collect information regularly from your library's customers about their interaction with the library. Here are some examples. You might put a survey on the front page of your library's website, asking respondents to tell you one thing that they would like you to improve about the website. You could put a survey at your circulation desk, asking respondents to tell you one thing that they liked about their visit to the library today. You could put two or three questions about the library in your newsletter, asking people to tell you about their most recent interaction with the library and what did and did not work in that experience. You could simply ask library users to tell you about their most recent interaction with the library, either in person or online, with the goal of beginning to develop your own journey map.

Once you have collected information from the library's users, think about how you might use that information to improve customer service. You may not have identified any specific issues, but did you gain a better understanding of how a particular type of person uses the library? If so, is there anything you can do to facilitate that type of interaction in the future and make it easier for the library user to get what he or she wants? Share what you have learned with your staff and leadership with the goal of gathering more information going forward.

Develop an adult user group, much like a teen user group, that will help you understand what customers want in terms of customer service. Ask for volunteers to meet on a regular schedule (once a month, four times a year, etc.). The goal of the group is to consider different aspects of customer service and provide their input about how the library might improve its customer service. Librarians could sign up to present ideas for new programs or services to this group and get their immediate input and ideas. When using a group of this size to collect input, remember that what you are hearing is directional not absolute, meaning that the group is too small in numbers to get anything but general ideas about how people might respond.

LEARNING

Reward people when they do customer service right. During my conversation with Chris, I asked how or if L.L.Bean rewarded employees who did a particularly good job at customer service. He said yes and then told me a story about when he started as an employee at L.L.Bean; he got the employee-of-the-month award for spending over five hours with two customers who walked in the door of the store and essentially wanted to buy everything they needed for a camping trip that they were embarking on that day. Chris did not just help them buy the equipment that they needed from his department. He then walked them from one area of the store to the next to make sure they got everything else they needed. The point I took away from this was not so much the details of the story as the fact that Chris very clearly remembered winning the award and what he had done to win, indicating that he was proud of winning the award. By rewarding employees this way, L.L.Bean is reinforcing the company's expectation about the need for company employees to provide exemplary customer service.

plcaton

eward library employees who go above and beyond in customer service. It does not really seem to matter whether you reward them with an employee-of-the-month award, a special parking space, or telling everyone in the library the story of what they did. What matters is that the library recognizes what the employee has done (thereby validating that behavior), and that by recognizing the employee, the story of what constitutes good customer service is shared across the organization.

▶ Idea

Put out a "Great Customer Service" box in your library and/or create a way for library patrons to e-mail examples of great customer service. Let library users know that if they encounter outstanding customer service to please put a note in the box, identifying the service performed and the library employee who provided it. Once a month, share and recognize this service with library employees. Talk about how the library customer perceived the interaction and why the experience meant something to that individual. It is important that employees remember that they are not the customers; just because a situation at the library does not bother them, this does not mean it will not bother a library customer. Another way to get librarians to "be the customer" is to ask them to use the library as patrons when they are not working. There is nothing like actually being a library user to give you a clear understanding of the quality of customer service at your library.

LEARNING

From a customer's perspective, the method by which you interact with the business (retail store, online, telephone) should not matter because the experience should be the same, regardless of the venue. L.L.Bean's goal is for *any* interaction with the customer to result in 100 percent satisfaction, regardless of how that interaction takes place. The company's website is just as important in this respect as a store visit or a telephone call. One experience should not be easier than another, nor should one be more complicated than another. And if a customer chooses to shop via one channel (like the catalog) but actually order through another channel (via the telephone), the experience should be as seamless as shopping through one channel. To support this perspective, L.L.Bean has an individual whose job title is, appropriately, Director of Omni Channel Customer Experience. That says it all!

▶ Implication

A library's users should be able to get what they need as easily online as they can by visiting the library in person and vice versa. Many librarians are thrilled just to be able to provide a working website with information about the libraries' activities and access to library databases. If something is not particularly smooth or easy to navigate, we tell ourselves, "That is okay because it is free" or "What do you expect given the lack of financial support for libraries in our state?" In a customer service–driven organization, this perspective is not valid. All experiences with the library need to be seamless, regardless of the venue. "Free" is no longer an excuse for "hard to figure out." Library customers have learned how easily they can get what they want from the open marketplace, and if they cannot have the same experience with the library, then they will go where they can get what they want, the way that they want it.

Libraries also need to start thinking about what happens if library users cannot get what they want, when they want it, the way that they want it. Those library users are going to start reacting like consumers in the open marketplace because the library has moved from "favored nation status" ("I'll put up with less than what I want") to just like every other organization out there ("I want what I want"). Here are some thoughts about what this can mean:

■ Unhappy library users will complain. According to the American Express 2012 Global Customer Service Barometer (http://about.americanexpress.com/news/docs/2012x/ axp_2012gcsb_us.pdf), Americans typically tell twenty-four people about negative customer service, and they tell only about fifteen people about positive experiences.

■ If customers are unhappy with their experience at the library, they will be less interested in having their tax dollars support the library and in continuing to use the library. According to the American Express 2011 Global Customer Service Barometer (http://about.americanexpress.com/news/docs/2011x/AXP_2011_csbar_us.pdf), seven in ten Americans said that they were willing to spend more with companies they believe provide excellent customer service. Also in 2011, according to a Customer Experience Impact Report by Oracle (www.oracle.com/us/products/applications/cust-exp-impact-report-epss-1560493.pdf), 86 percent of consumers quit doing business with a company because of a bad customer experience.

The impact of poor customer service is real and powerful.

► Idea

Identify five to ten aspects of customer service that your library sees as universal, meaning that library users should experience those aspects of customer service whether they are in the library building or using some of the library's digital resources. Then, develop a short customer survey asking your library's users to rank their experience on the library's website, on its social media pages, and in the brick-and-mortar building with respect to each of those universal elements. Your scores will help you understand where you need to start making adjustments and improvements in customer service.

LEARNING

Having the right technology can help drive customer service to a higher level of excellence. In an environment that pledges to provide the same level of customer service, regardless of how the customer is "touching" L.L.Bean, it has become critical to have the right technology to facilitate this level of customer support. L.L.Bean uses simple technology in its retail stores to allow employees to get fast answers to customer questions. It uses more complicated technology to collect customer information and store it so it can be accessed when needed. It employs highly sophisticated technology to take in customer comments and understand the implications of such for its business. In the near future, the company will be launching apps that will allow customers to use their mobile phones to get information about a product in a store just by scanning it. The company has won awards for developing a website that is easy to use and navigate and within which customers can get answers to most of their questions without ever having to talk directly to a person—but if they want to talk to a person, that is easy to do also. Bottom line: L.L.Bean does not just say it is customer focused; the company also spends the money to put the technology in place to support this ethic from every angle. If a customer comes into the store and wants to buy a sweater for his wife, just like the one she got several years ago at L.L.Bean, the store has the technology and database that will allow them help the customer do just that. And when the company develops technology platforms, it starts with customers' needs and builds the technology to address those needs.

► Implication

To be truly customer focused, a library needs to put the infrastructure in place to support this work, and that infrastructure needs to be up-to-date, not old and glitchy. Libraries are in a critical battle to prove that they are relevant and can meet the needs of their communities. If people walk into the library assuming that it can help them with their technology or guide them in finding information only to discover that the librarians cannot help them because they are working with old, ineffective equipment, then the needs of the customers have not been met and confidence will be low about how much the library can actually accomplish. Librarians need to understand and be very adept at using the current consumer marketplace technology if they are to have any sort of ability to provide real customer service. This is somewhat like the situation that local police forces have found themselves in over the past ten years in the United States. In many small towns, criminals have better, more effective weapons than the local police. How can the police force do their job effectively if they do not even have the right equipment? Similarly, how can librarians do their jobs correctly if they do not know how to help their customers use the latest consumer technology?

▶ Idea

If your library does not have up-to-date technology and/or equipment, survey your library patrons about what level of customer service they think is being provided. Write a grant or do fund-raising to get the funds to upgrade at least some elements of your technology. Then, do a postsurvey, again focusing on customer service. The odds are very good that your library's customer service rating will improve fairly dramatically because now your librarians are able to provide the service that these patrons want—help in using today's technology. You now have a case study to help you get better ongoing funding for technology to support customer service. I know this requires a commitment of time and people to make a project like this happen, but the result (a compelling case as to why technology matters in the library) can make a real difference in a library's ability to provide truly outstanding customer service.

LEARNING

Develop a clear process to figure out how to use the information that you get from and about customers. One of the questions that I raised with Chris was how L.L.Bean deals with the input of information that they get every day about their customers. All I could think was how on earth could anyone manage to get a handle on any small portion of that? He identified the following points as key in L.L.Bean's ability to do this:

- You must have an organization that is alert, adaptive, and responsive. The organization as a whole must be able to filter out the "noise" that comes in with that much information and at the same time identify when that noise has the potential to grow into a major opportunity or issue.
- The organization must be very clear about its overall goals to help build an automatic prioritization when it comes to weeding the information.

▪ L.L.Bean keeps track of all of the products with identified issues through what is called a product enhancement backlog. This allows them to identify issues without having to jump right in to fix the issues until the time is right. This keeps the organization focused on priorities even when they get information saying a product is not working correctly.

▶ Implication

Before a library starts to collect information from and about its patrons, it should develop a plan for managing and using what it learns. Because information about library patrons is private and because libraries are committed to supporting that privacy, it is critical to plan (a) how you will collect information voluntarily from donors and (b) what you will do with any customer information collected to ensure it remains confidential and is only used in an appropriate fashion. How will that information be stored and how can the library guarantee the privacy of library users? Privacy is a concept that is rapidly disappearing in today's digital environment, but libraries do not want to do anything that will increase the speed with which this happens. There are ways that libraries can do this. For example, they can commit to collecting only anonymous information, and they can eliminate the risk of a computer being hacked for information by putting user data only on a computer with no Internet access that is kept in a locked office. Bottom line: there is a great deal of information that libraries can collect and keep about their patrons that will not imperil our commitment to supporting their privacy.

In addition, libraries should plan to define carefully how they will use any information that they do collect. Today's computer users are generally savvy to the fact that companies collect and use information about them. What they do not like is when that information is given or sold to third-party companies without their authorization. So, if libraries are going to collect information about their users, they need to tell them how they will use that information, the benefit to the library of getting that information, and the ultimate benefit to the user by sharing that information (better library services and products).

▶ Idea

If your library is considering collecting patron data to help support better customer service, start by reviewing how businesses communicate with their customers about their use of customer data. Businesses are becoming more and more concerned about reassuring customers that information about them is not being sold or misused. They have spent a great deal of time and money to develop language around this issue to help make sure customers are comfortable sharing their data. You can learn from how businesses do this and then apply it to your own situation as appropriate.

LEARNING

Agile development helps identify problems and implement relatively small changes before big fixes become needed. Agile development is another way to articulate the concept of test, test, test, and fail quickly (see chapter 2). It means that a company does less major product development that requires large amounts of time and resources and does more "product tuning." Product tuning means that L.L.Bean focuses on addressing a customer problem that has been identified, iterating potential solutions to be tested in two- to four-week cycles. After a potential solution is tried, it is evaluated in terms of what did and did not work, and then the process starts again. The idea is that by working in short cycles, failure is actually a good thing because it lets you identify the problem and fix it for the next two-week cycle. The problems identified in these short time periods are generally relatively inexpensive and can be easily fixed. In comparison, traditional product development can take years and failure in those situations can be financially devastating for a company.

▶ Implication

Libraries can use the concept of product tuning in the development of new community services. Product tuning means that you develop and release new products and services more quickly than is traditional at libraries and then plan to adjust and fix problems as you go along. This means that libraries are able to do much more exploration and discovery than if they only put out perfect programs and services.

A product-tuning approach also means that you make mistakes as you go and that the people who use your library may encounter some of these mistakes as they try out new services. Given the focus of this chapter on customer service, is this the best way to deliver customer service? I think that this process actually improves customer service if you do it the right way. You need to ensure that your library users understand that some products and services are "in development" and may have glitches associated with using them, but they are available anyway because you wanted them to have access to them as quickly as possible. Ask for their thoughts about the products/services. What do they like and what does not work? If you incorporate the input of your library patrons, let them know. This is a great way of directly demonstrating that you hear what they have to say and will act on it—and that is customer service in a nutshell.

▶ Idea

Hang a large sheet of paper in the entry to your library to solicit feedback from patrons. Across the top of the paper, write out an idea that you have for a new service or program at your library. Provide sticky notepads and pens on a table next to the paper. Ask the members of your community to tell you what they like and dislike about the idea and what (if anything) they might do differently. After three days of (hopefully) substantial input, take down the paper, look at the responses, and adjust the concept based on the input. Repost the paper and ask for feedback a second time. Rewrite the concept one more time after three more days of input. Ask your patrons to grade the end result on a scale. The goal of this idea is not necessarily to develop a new program for your library (although you might decide that you want to use the end result of the exercise). Rather, the goal is to understand how product tuning works and to internalize the extent to which it can truly add value in a very short period of time.

LEARNING

Giving consumers the opportunity to try out products and services can increase their satisfaction with both. L.L.Bean has developed the Outdoor Discovery Learning program as a cornerstone of its philosophy of "learn, try, buy, enjoy." To participate, consumers sign up for short programs to try out a new outdoor activity and the equipment associated with that activity. The company believes that providing the experiences that go with the products that they sell enhances the overall L.L.Bean experience for the customer. The concept is called experiential retail because the retailer has provided the customer with a way to try out or experience products and services in a setting that gives them a sense of how they will work in the real world. L.L.Bean does this in its stores also by providing small hills to go up and down in hiking boots to figure out if they are comfortable. The company plans days throughout the summer when you can go to a nearby body of water to try out different kayaks that you are thinking about purchasing. You can take a fishing rod outside and try casting on the lawn in front of the stores (developed for that purpose). All of these methods are ways to help a potential customer experience an outdoor environment and try out L.L.Bean's equipment in that environment to see if it will meet his or her needs. This is really the ultimate in customer service even while it helps the sales of L.L.Bean products.

▶ Implication

Libraries can use the experiential retail concept to bring more users into the library and at the same time provide better customer service. If the library building is clean, open, and inviting and has new things regularly happening in it, it becomes a magnet for people to come in to see what is going on. At the same time that these elements draw people into the building, they also provide improved customer service to the patrons already using the building.

▶ Idea

Near the entrance to your library, develop an experiential "quick stop." The quick stop is basically a thematic book display with an experiential element attached to it that changes on a regular basis. For example, you might have a display about crafting books available in the library, and as part of that display, you could provide knitting needles and yarn and one sheet of paper that tells patrons how to start knitting, or you could do a nautical-themed display and provide ropes and a how-to sheet about tying boating knots. The idea is to add an experiential element to book displays that you already do with the goal of attracting people into the library and providing better customer service through better experiences.

LEARNING

People do not have much free time in today's world, so you need to create an environment where they will enjoy spending time. This was Chris's response when I asked him what he would do to make Curtis Library more customer oriented. I knew immediately what he meant when he said this. At the L.L.Bean store in Freeport, Maine, they have stocked trout in two different locations in the store to help you feel the ambiance of being out in the woods of Maine. You are encouraged to try out equipment in the L.L.Bean stores. Customer service is outstanding. There are places in the stores where you can sit and rest when you are shopping. When you go into L.L.Bean's discount store, you can find canoes filled with products on sale or tents that are set up on the floor of the store. Generally, you just plain enjoy going into these stores. If people do not have much free time in their lives, why would they choose to use what they do have going to a location that is not enjoyable?

▶ Implication

If libraries want their customers to spend time in the library, then they need to provide a welcoming, inviting space where people want to be and where new things are happening on a regular basis to make the trip worth their time. The library that I used when I was growing up never changed. When I would go back to my hometown for a visit, the library felt exactly like it did when I was using it as a child. There were no displays about books or any other topics, and any art in the library had been there for a thousand years (well, it felt that way to me). If that were the case today, would you use the library for anything more than running in to get something to read and running out again? I am guessing that the answer for most people is no. People want to spend their spare time in a welcoming space that invites them in and provides great customer service.

Chris reinforced this idea with me in a way that really grabbed my attention. As I was walking Chris out of the library at the end of our interview, we were discussing how you make retail stores attractive and inviting. Chris took one look at the security gates in my library and asked me, "Do you think those gates help create an inviting environment where people want to hang out?" Gulp. Good point. I am not sure what the end result will be with my library's security gates, but his comment about them really drove home for me how L.L.Bean employees look at *everything* that might have an impact on customer service.

▶ Idea

Ask library employees, for one week, to walk in the same doors that library patrons use and to spend five minutes just looking around at the different parts of the library. At the end of the week, ask them to identify one thing that makes the space unwelcoming or that provides poor customer service. They are not focusing on the customer service provided by people at the library but rather the extent to which ancillary equipment and spaces meet the needs of customers. Ask them to provide any ideas they might have about how the issues they identify could be resolved with the end goal being improved customer service.

• THE BIG IDEAS FROM THIS INTERVIEW •

I think the most transformative concept that I discovered in my discussion with Chris Wilson is not one piece of learning but instead is the degree of focus that L.L.Bean puts on customer service. It really is part of everything they do, and it does seem to drive their decision making on both the little and big issues in the company. What I took away from that was how much more libraries could do to drive customer service in their organizations.

The learning "From a customer's perspective, the method by which you interact with the business (retail store, online, telephone) should not matter because the experience should be the same, regardless of the venue" has great potential to change how libraries operate. For so many years, we have assumed that libraries are not held to the same standard as retailers and so it is okay if their customer interactions are not as polished as retailers', especially online. However, customers are learning to expect through their retail experiences that the channel of interaction should not matter, and they are transferring that expectation to all of their customer service interactions, including those with libraries. This means that now libraries do need to assume that they are being held to the same expectations as retailers, which means that most libraries have some work to do to bring up the standards of their online services.

The last piece of learning that I think is particularly powerful is not new at all—"People do not have much free time in today's world, so you need to create an environment where they will enjoy spending time." In fact, this statement seems pretty obvious. However, I had always thought that if I created a clean, safe, pleasant library environment that people would automatically spend more time in the library. This learning brought me up short because it made me realize that libraries are in competition with every other resource in the community for the very limited free time that people have to spend outside their jobs and their personal lives. I am not sure I have an answer for this one—it is more of a wake-up call to me!

• SUMMARY OF WHAT I LEARNED •

- In an organization that is committed to being customer-centric, clear and concise communication ensures that everyone understands what this means.
- In a truly customer-centric organization, the first question asked in all situations becomes "What is the right thing to do for the customer?"
- The process of knowing your customers and understanding what they want from your business never stops.

- Reward people when they do customer service right.
- From a customer's perspective, the method by which you interact with the business (retail store, online, telephone) should not matter because the experience should be the same, regardless of the venue.
- Having the right technology can help drive customer service to a higher level of excellence.
- Develop a clear process to figure out how to use the information that you get from and about customers.
- Agile development helps identify problems and implement relatively small changes before big fixes become needed.
- Giving consumers the opportunity to try out products and services can increase their satisfaction with both.
- People do not have much free time in today's world, so you need to create an environment where they will enjoy spending time.

• RESOURCES •

The Effortless Experience: Conquering the New Battleground for Customer Loyalty, by Matthew Dixon (Portfolio Hardcover, 2013)

The Future of Customer Service, September 2014 Trend Briefing, Trendwatching.com (the subject of chapter 7 in this book), http://trendwatching.com/trends/future-customer-service

"Using Customer Journey Maps to Improve Customer Experience," by Adam Richardson, *Harvard Business Review*, November 15, 2010, https://hbr.org/2010/11/using-customer-journey-maps-to

• INTERVIEW QUESTIONS •

How do you define outstanding customer success at L.L.Bean?

What do you think are the key attributes of a customer-centric organization?

Do you think quick resolution of issues is as important to good customer service as making the customer "always right"?

Do you think there is a point at which customers should ever be "fired"?

How do you institutionalize outstanding customer service as a key cultural norm?

How do you get L.L.Bean employees to be customer centered even when no one is looking?

What role does L.L.Bean leadership take in institutionalizing customer service?

Do you get input from your customers about customer service? How does it get shared in the organization?

What are the hardest parts of providing excellent customer service and how do you address those issues?

What are the easiest parts of customer service for staff? What makes them easy?

How do you get departments that are not customer facing to focus on customer service?

How do you hire people who you think will provide outstanding customer service?

Do you reward staff for outstanding customer service and, if so, how? Do you try to reward in such a way as to motivate staff or recognize staff?

What sort of training do you do about customer service and how often does it happen?

How do ideas get surfaced for improving customer service?

How do you know when you are being successful with respect to providing outstanding customer service?

What is the worst thing that you can do to a customer? How do you make sure that does not happen in your organization?

How often does customer service get discussed at L.L.Bean?

What tips would you share with an organization that wants to be customer-centric?

Do you have any books or other resources that you would recommend as "must reads" for libraries interested in focusing on customer service?

7

TREND TRACKING

VICKI LOOMIS
Trendwatching.com

• WHY THIS TOPIC •

Trend tracking has been of interest to me for years. It is such a useful way of evaluating and understanding what is happening in the world that I have always seen it as a powerful tool. I wrote an article for *American Libraries* magazine about the topic (www.americanlibrariesmagazine.org/article/10-tips-tracking-trends), and I have done many presentations about it to libraries. Trend tracking is easy to execute, it is interesting, and it can be immediately helpful to libraries, making it a useful endeavor. My goal in exploring this topic in this book is to examine the concept further, understand how the experts do it, and continue to espouse its value as a tool for the library profession.

Sometimes when I do presentations about trend tracking, I am asked why libraries should look at trends outside their environment. What relevance can consumer trends have to how the local public library operates? My response is that consumer trends are wonderful indicators of what is important to the same people who also use our libraries. If libraries understand what needs and wants people are trying to fulfill through the purchase of consumer products, they will inevitably start to see ways in which they can fulfill some of those needs and wants. To quote Trendwatching .com, "Consumers don't live inside industry silos. Neither should you."

• WHY THIS ORGANIZATION •

Trendwatching.com, established in 2002, was one of the first organizations to start doing trend spotting in an organized fashion and today has more than 2,600 trend spotters around the world who share the trends they see developing. The company has a tremendous understanding of how to see trends, how to determine what trends mean, and how to develop ideas for businesses based on those trends. The Trendwatching .com website provides an extensive library of information, updated monthly, about new trends and ideas about how to use those trends. The work featured on the website is practical, interesting, and very accessible to the average reader, so I am an advocate of sending people who are interested in learning more about trends in the company's direction. Vicki Loomis, who works in Trendwatching.com's London office, and I had a wonderful conversation about how the company operates, how trends indicate what is happening in the retail and nonprofit environments, and how libraries might do more to use trends.

• INSIGHTS FROM THIS INTERVIEW •

LEARNING

A consumer trend is a new expression of what people need, want, or expect from the products and services that they use in their lives. A trend is not something that just happens without any context. Rather, "trends emerge when external change unlocks new ways to serve age-old human needs and desires" (http://trendwatching.com/trends/instant-trend-expert). For example, people have always wanted human interaction and connection, and the widespread use of social media is a trend that has happened because technology has provided new ways to satisfy that age-old human need.

One of the most powerful parts of trend hunting is that the process of identifying trends helps the observer understand the underlying human need being addressed. Once that need is recognized, organizations can start to consider how they might provide products and services to address that need themselves. Trends address basic needs, so once they are established they tend to stick around until a better way develops to address the same needs. Fads, on the other hand, are based more on fancy or whim; they tend to be short-lived and have very little relationship to human needs.

▶ Implication

Trends are leading indicators of change that libraries can use to inform their decisions about products and services they choose to offer. Trends indicate that some sort of change has happened to support a new way of meeting a basic human need. Therefore, understanding the trends that are evolving gives libraries a way to see change coming and to figure out how they can prepare themselves to address that change. If you look for trends, you will see the wave building and can figure out how to ride that wave. Without trend spotting, it is much easier to get swamped by a wave when it hits you unexpectedly.

At a practical level, trends are the early warning signals for what happens in our communities. When you see a trend start to develop, you know that groups of people are reacting to something that is happening and they are reacting in the same way. By monitoring trends, libraries can start to be more aware of what is happening in the communities they serve and this, in turn, will help them decide if they want to respond to a trend with library services and products.

▶ Idea

Start tracking trends. How can you do this without having it take too much of your time, energy, or funds? The following are some simple, inexpensive, and easy ways to start understanding trends, as suggested by Vicki during our conversation:

- Sign up for a dedicated Twitter account that will exist only to help you see trends developing. Once you get the account, follow people whom you see as being influential in your community. Make a point of reading their tweets on a regular basis. Do you start seeing the same ideas being articulated by multiple individuals or groups? Do those ideas get picked up by other people and shared so that the number of people who are aware of them grows? If so, then a trend is starting.

- Use a similar approach with any available news outlets that you can "follow" (following makes collecting information easier because it comes to you and you do not have to search it out), looking at news feeds and reading blogs.

- Follow futurists and big thinkers, not just in the library profession but in any industry that you find interesting. These are folks who make their living identifying trends, and generally they share much of what they discover. You can also learn by looking at *how* they identify trends. I follow Thomas Frey and Stephen Abram, both interesting writers with a lot to say about libraries in the future, and Faith Popcorn, who operates in the consumer marketplace and has been defining trends in that environment for years.

Keep the process of trend spotting going for at least three months. During this period, question yourself regularly: What do I see happening that is being mirrored in multiple locations? How might I take this idea and apply it to libraries? Are there any limitations, meaning what can you reasonably do with the idea? At the end of three months, evaluate what you have discovered to determine if you are starting to see trends develop and to get ideas about how to use those trends.

LEARNING

Learning to identify consumer trends can help make sense of the deluge of information available in today's environment and can provide a framework by which to understand rapid change. Identifying trends allows you to process and focus, helping you sort through the mounds of ideas and information that come at you every day by providing a framework on which you can hang those ideas/trends and start to understand what they say about the changes happening in our environment. In other words, tracking trends can help you keep your head above water when you get swamped by all of the information being churned out in today's world (to carry my water analogies a bit further). It gives you a way to group and sort information, connect different ideas, and start to understand the implications of such.

Trendwatching.com provides a tool, a consumer trend canvas, to help trend spotters do this work (http://trendwatching.com/trends/consumertrendcanvas). The basic process is simple but very effective. You start by evaluating the trend to identify the basic human need that is being addressed by the trend. Step two is to look at the broader context of the trend with the goal of understanding why that trend is emerging now. What has changed both long term and short term to facilitate the evolution of that trend? Step three is to consider the emerging consumer expectations that are developing as a result of these changes in the environment. Step four is to understand how other organizations are addressing the trend that is evolving. Finally, after developing a thorough understanding of the trend and what is driving its development, the last step is to consider how your organization could meet the consumer needs and expectations identified in the first steps and who you think might be interested in that product or service if you developed it. One person can go through this process or a team of people can work through it. I think the most effective method is to have a team start the process and then send the individual members of the team away to think about and build on the ideas that came from their brainstorming. Then, have the team meet one more time to work on one another's ideas together.

▶ Implication

Trend tracking can help libraries start to see multiple trends moving in the same direction and addressing the same issue, which may indicate a need for libraries to change or adjust how they serve their communities. Individual trends are not going to provide you with magical insights into what people want in their lives. However, if libraries start to see several trends addressing the same opportunity or need, then it is clear that a basic human need is changing and the marketplace is recognizing and reacting to that change.

For example, Trendingwatching.com has identified a trend called "sympathetic pricing," which is defined as "flexible and imaginative discounts that help ease lifestyle pain points, lend a helping hand in difficult times, or support a shared value" (http://trendwatching .com/trends/sympathetic-pricing). The company notes that although brands are constantly telling consumers that they care about them, the consumers do not believe this. In reaction, brands are finding small ways to demonstrate that they really do care about consumers and the small issues in their lives. Examples include a hotel chain in Australia that provides discounts for rainy days during a visitor's stay and a restaurant that provides free drinks on Thursday nights for patrons who walk in the door with a parking ticket.

If a library knew about this trend, what might it do to reinforce that the local library cares about its community? How about eliminating fines if library users bring in canned goods for the local food bank (which is becoming a trend in libraries)? How about eliminating overdue fines completely? Or, what if your library used overdue fines specifically for a program that addressed a basic need in your community, like holding adult literacy classes or providing seeds for a community garden to feed the homeless? If the basic human need in this scenario is that people want to know that organizations really do care when they say that they do, what other ways might a library demonstrate this? Libraries assume that people know their local library cares about the community, but it is important never to be complacent. And the people in your community who do not use the library may not have that perspective, so a little love can never hurt.

▶ Idea

Spend a month developing a process that helps you see and understand the trends developing in your local community. Do this by reading local newspapers, liking Facebook pages of local institutions (e.g., the library or senior center or sports center), following tweets from Twitter accounts of local people-in-the-know, and listening to local talk radio. Learn to scan your environment constantly, searching for the indicators of trends developing. When you see something that looks interesting, think about whether what you are seeing relates in any way to other trends that you have seen developing. Start looking at some of the online trend-spotting websites (see this chapter's Resources for suggestions). Why keep an eye on national as well as local trends? In the long run, national trends become local trends if they truly have staying power. The goal is to develop a trend-spotting method that works for you and helps you keep a constant finger on the pulse of your library's community.

LEARNING

The skills required to identify trends include curiosity and the ability to consider why something is happening, how events connect and interact, and what need is being fulfilled by the trend. If you are a curious (nosy?) person, trend hunting is fun. You see something happening, wonder why, and then go searching for answers. You enjoy not just seeing the new ideas popping up in the marketplace but also understanding why they are happening and determining if there are any correlations among them. Trend spotters tend to read across a wide variety of topics because they like to learn a little bit about a lot. Natural-born trend spotters are always scanning the world to see what is new and different, and they are fascinated by what causes people to do what they do.

▶ Implication

Librarians are natural-born trend spotters. Librarians are curious people who love to find answers to questions. They are also pit bulls about not giving up until they figure out the answers to their questions. The biggest challenge in getting library employees to start trend hunting is to overcome their perspective that this is more work. It is not. Essentially, to be a good trend hunter, you simply have to remember what you see and then start thinking about potential connections. If you already do this and enjoy it, then you are a natural trend spotter.

The following is the process that I share with people who are intrigued by trend hunting and want to try it out; it is simple and it works:

1. Stop, look, and listen. Follow professional trend spotters. Read popular press. Watch commercial television. Gather as much input as you can about what is happening in our consumer society.

2. Look for patterns and connections. Keep track of ideas that pop into your head. Look for repetition in words and ideas. Look for similar patterns of behavior. Listen to your intuition when it tells you that you have seen this before and it means something.

3. Identify the trend. Again, look for similar patterns. Are they saying the same thing? What do you think is going on? What basic human need is being addressed? Has there been some sort of change that has allowed a new way to address this need to evolve? Summarize what you think is happening.

4. Brainstorm implications. What effect might the trend have on your community? Is it likely to be a big, important trend that will affect a lot of people and have long-term ramifications? If the trend seems important, how might your library respond in a way that will be helpful to your community? Or is it an interesting trend but probably not all that important?

5. Let the ideas percolate. Ask for input from others. Consider whether you have any experts who might provide a helpful perspective.

6. Finalize and summarize your idea.

7. Get buy-in, get funding, and get to work!

▶ Ideas

Ask library employees to read the free, monthly Trend Briefings provided on the Trendwatching.com website. Spend five minutes once a month at a staff meeting talking about what library staff got out of each report. Do they agree with the trend identified? What examples of that trend do they see in your community or in the larger world community? Do they have any ideas about how the library might use that trend to improve some aspect of library services? Being more conscious of trends as they are happening will help library employees consider how the library might use those trends to improve its services.

Hold a brown-bag lunch training session during which employees learn the process of "unpacking" a trend using Trendwatching.com's consumer trend canvas method. I think the easiest way to learn how to use trends is to be involved in the process of spotting them and then figuring out whether or not they have relevance for your organization. Training gives everyone the opportunity to understand how trend spotting works, and, if necessary, the staff involved can adjust the trend-watching process so that it works more effectively for them.

LEARNING

What happens to consumers in one place affects their expectations in others. As expressed by Vicki during our discussion, the online world is shaping our offline expectations. Consumers are rapidly getting used to a certain level of experience online. They can find the products and services they want no matter how esoteric in nature. The process of shopping for products is simple, and online there are often tools that are not available offline, programs that find the cheapest prices or the best product option. Products and services are generally delivered quickly and without complications. Pricing is reasonable online, and you often have many more options from which to choose. Why would consumers expect anything different when they are out in the brick-and-mortar world? They see no reason why their in-store experience should not be just as fluid, seamless, and simple as their online experience.

▶ Implication

Libraries can no longer offer services and products that are "good enough" because they are free or because they are the best they can do with a limited budget. The Internet has resulted in a global community where ideas can go around the world literally in one afternoon and where new products and services can be reviewed and either succeed or fail within a twenty-four-hour period. Libraries no longer live and operate in a vacuum. Consumers' experiences online, in stores, at school, at work, and in their homes all affect their expectations when they walk into the local community library.

Today's consumers judge services across industries and across channels of distribution. What they learn in one place about customer service they take with them to every customer service experience they have. What they experience on their Amazon Kindle with respect to reading e-books they take with them to every digital reading experience (including at the library) that they have. If libraries cannot measure up to consumers' expectations, they will be discarded. This is especially true with people in their twenties and thirties who have grown up in a world driven by technology and who simply assume that online standards of service apply everywhere.

How many times has your library struggled for months to decide if you should provide a new service (like e-books)? Then, once you finally decide to offer a product, you more often than not have to figure out how to pay for it, determine where it will be located in the library, and decide which staff members will be responsible for managing it. When the product finally gets launched, everyone breathes a huge sigh of relief because now the library is competitive with the marketplace. However, in the six months it took you to go through all of that, the marketplace has moved on to the next new thing and now you have to start all over again. We need to stop operating this way and get ahead of these new ideas so that, instead of reacting to them, we can evaluate them and then determine if we want to offer them to our library consumers.

▶ Idea

Evaluate any digital service offered by your library by comparing it to a similar service offered for profit. So, if you offer streaming movies, compare the service that your library provides to that of Netflix or Hulu. Ask yourself the following questions:

■ Is the library's service as easy to sign up for as the commercial service?

- Can you get the movies that you want in the same amount of time that you can get them from a commercial provider?
- Are the same movies available?
- Are the movies as easy to return as they are to the commercial provider?
- What costs, if any, are associated with keeping the movies for longer than the borrowing period?

If the service offered by the library for any of these standards differs from a commercial option, ask yourself whether the degree of difference is worth the value provided. If not, consider how you can improve the library's service so that it is at least equal to, if not better than, that provided by the commercial enterprise.

But, you say to yourself, "I can't spend as much as Hulu or Netflix does to provide my service. My budgets are constrained more and more every year. How can I compete?" I think the answer is that we have to compete, but we need to pick and choose where we compete. Originally, my expectation as a library director was that if there was a new technology or product in the market, I wanted to have it available at the library. However, I have now reached the perspective that this does not always make sense. Libraries cannot afford to keep up with the extraordinary pace of change happening in technology and consumer product development. Instead, my future goal is to specialize by providing only those digital services which are as good as (or better than) what the library's users can get commercially. By providing niche products and services, I can make sure that what I do provide is the best, and there is certainly a place for that in consumers' minds. We do not want our libraries to become the standard of mediocrity ("I'll go to the library only if I can't get what I want any other way") when we really want them to be the standard of excellence.

LEARNING

When big brands make changes in how they do business, it affects everyone. This is another way of articulating the interconnectedness of all things in today's world. Big brands have an impact with a large radius. And if consumers start seeing something they like happening with big brands, then they will start to expect the same from little brands and nonprofits and pretty much every organization with which they interact. The good part about this is that you can see trends developing in a market just by watching what the big brands do and how consumers respond. Think about McDonald's and its move to a healthier menu; the minute McDonald's did it, every other fast-food chain in town did the same thing. Consumers loved the change, and now having salads on fast-food menus is considered to be standard. Watching the big guys is another way to trend spot simply and easily.

▶ Implication

Libraries need to start thinking about how the actions of big businesses might affect how they operate. Think about the previous McDonald's example. If you were aware that McDonald's and then other fast-food manufacturers were responding to a consumer desire for better food, how might that affect the library? You might purchase materials to inform library patrons about health and nutrition, you might develop programs around the topic of healthy eating on a small budget, and you might even consider partnering with McDonald's to do a presentation on why they responded to consumer trends in the way that they did. The first two examples are probably quite obvious to most librarians. The last idea of partnering with McDonald's probably made everyone who was reading this twitch. Libraries do not work with businesses! Well, why not? If we can help library patrons by working with businesses, then we should consider working with them.

▶ Idea

For one month, as you read newspapers and magazines, keep looking for information about what big business is doing. Keep a log of what you find. As you identify trends, think about how your library might respond to those trends. As I was writing this book, I saw a perfect example of this in the news: Apple Computer will be introducing the Apple

Watch in 2015. What does this have to do with libraries? Apple is a trendsetter. Remember the iPod and the revolution that it started? If Apple is going to come out with a watch in 2015, you can bet that it will set off a whole new wave of technology development in response. Smart libraries will start to analyze this product and the trend it represents with the goal of understanding not *if* it will affect libraries but *how* it will affect libraries. The following is an example of how a library might start to think about the shadow that this particular big brand will throw across library operations:

- The Apple Watch is being developed to personalize technology. You can purchase the standard Apple Watch, an Apple Sport Watch, or the Apple Watch Edition. There are (according to Apple) more than two million ways to personalize the Apple Watch face to meet your needs and specifications. People can get their technology and make a statement about who they are by how they do it (as though being an Apple person versus a PC person is not already seen as a fashion statement). Libraries, on the other hand, provide the most basic access to technology with no ability for users of library computers to personalize them or how they work. The Apple Watch could be the precursor to the demise of the standard, sterile library computer lab. Should we start addressing this possibility and, if so, how?
- The Apple Watch is the ultimate in making technology immediately available. You do not have to pull it out of a pocket, you do not have to plug it in, and it is always right there for you. It addresses the basic human need for connection by making it easier to do it at any moment. The Apple Watch is the ultimate on-the-go technology. If the Apple Watch becomes a mainstream consumer technology, it will mean that technology has taken a huge step toward being primarily mobile. Apps will eventually be developed for only mobile technology, making library computers obsolete. What responsibility will libraries have in terms of making mobile technology available to their communities to ensure access?

LEARNING

Market research looks at what has happened, whereas consumer trends are forward thinking about where things could go next. In my previous career as a marketer, I learned a great deal about market research and its importance in helping people make decisions about their businesses. I wanted to understand the difference between doing market research and doing trend spotting. Was trend spotting a better tool to help organizations understand what to do with their businesses? Vicki's response was that essentially market research looks at the past—what has already happened. Understanding what has happened can sometimes help you figure out where to go moving forward, but just as often, "past performance is not necessarily an indicator of future performance." In addition, market research is limited by what consumers are able to articulate about what they want. This is not to say that market research has no value. It can be a very helpful tool to understand a marketplace, but it is limited in scope.

In comparison, spotting consumer trends is a way of thinking about the future—what might happen going forward. If you become adept at trend spotting, you can start to see things that consumers want but probably could not articulate to you that they want. Having a future orientation in your research means that you can use what you learn to help you identify new directions for future programs and products in the library.

▶ Implication

Trend spotting is the perfect tool for libraries to help them define their future. Market research is a tool that I use when I want to understand how our community perceives what the library has done in the past. Trend hunting gives me a tool to plan for the future. It helps me understand what is happening in the broader environment that could have an impact on how the library operates. In addition, it gives me the methodology for finding new ideas that can take advantage of specific trends and keep the library ahead of what is happening, instead of reacting to something that has already happened.

▶ Idea

Using the Apple Watch example cited earlier, brainstorm about what consumer needs you see being addressed by these products and the impact you think these trends might have on your library. Can your library respond to the trends that you identify with its own products and services? Are there any products and services that you would eliminate or change because of the trends that you identify? Could your library be affected in any unique way (compared to other libraries) by this trend? After you have gone through this with the Apple Watch, look at fast-food restaurants. Are there any trends happening there that you think might ultimately have an impact on your library? How about the car industry?

LEARNING

Trend spotting can be a low-cost tool for organizations. Trend spotting is not expensive. It is something that anyone can learn, and it requires only that you keep your eyes open and be curious about what you see happening. Trend spotters need to think about why something is happening, to look below the surface of the event and think about what is causing the event to occur. They need to think about what need is being fulfilled and what change has occurred that now allows that need to be addressed in a unique way. Trendwatching.com has thousands of trend spotters around the world who act in this capacity primarily because they are interested in trends.

▶ Implication

Trend spotting is an inexpensive way for libraries to start identifying and understanding how trends can affect their future. Trend spotting costs only time and the desire to do the research involved. Time is hard to find at most libraries, but the more you can turn trend spotting into a habit that you do all the time versus a project that you have to stop your real work to do, the more useful it will become. The other great thing about trend spotting is that it is something anyone in the library can do. There is no special education needed to do trend spotting, just some time learning the basic techniques. Being a good trend spotter is more about an interest and attitude than it is a particular skill set. This means that anyone in an organization who has the time and/or inclination can become the official trend spotter.

▶ Ideas

Offer training on trend spotting and make it available to any library employee or volunteer who expresses an interest. The Trendwatching.com website offers plenty of content to develop a curriculum for trend spotting. You should also feel free to use my "Trend Tracking" presentation, available on my blog (http://irreverentlibrarian.wordpress.com/presentations). It was developed specifically to help library staff understand how to become trend hunters. However, keep in mind that once you train people to become trend spotters, then you need to start planning how you are going to keep track of what they discover and put it to use for your library's benefit.

Use a Request for Project Consideration form to convince your library's leadership to try out ideas initiated by trend research. The basic idea of the Request for Project Consideration (RFPC) is that it will help you develop a short, concise, articulate rationale to convince your library's leadership to try out an idea that evolves from your trend research. This is a tool that I learned about in the Simmons MLS program from Professor Bob Dugan, and I shared my version of it in my last book *What They Don't Teach You in Library School* (ALA Editions, 2010). I received a lot of feedback that it has been an exceptionally useful tool for librarians across the country, so I think it is worth reiterating here. The RFPC is one sheet of paper or less. It is never longer than one page because the goal of this document is to be short and concise. If it takes you more than one page to summarize your argument, then you need to rethink your argument.

The RFPC starts with a summary of the project idea. The second point is to identify where the idea originated. This section helps the reader understand if the idea just floated in the door or if there was research that went into developing it. Third, identify the costs associated with the project concept. Next, identify a topline timetable so the reader understands how long it will take to bring the idea to fruition. Follow this by identifying library resources that will be needed to execute the project. Then (and very important), identify any potential issues around implementation that you are aware of at this point in time. Finally, tell the reader how you are going to measure success if you have the opportunity to execute the project.

That is the entire document. You do not want to spend hours and hours developing it, but at the same time, you do want to put enough time and energy into it to demonstrate that you have done the homework to provide reliable information. If you get approval for the concept, you already have a framework to help you start putting together a project plan. If you do not get approval, you can ask for specific feedback to tell you which part of the project is not convincing the reader to support its development. This, in turn, makes it easier to go back and adjust the RFPC so that it will be approved the second time. This is a great tool to use with ideas germinated out of trend spotting, but it can be used equally effectively when requesting support for other types of projects.

• THE BIG IDEAS FROM THIS INTERVIEW •

Two learnings that came out of this interview I think have the potential to change how libraries think and operate. The first is "What happens to consumers in one place affects their expectations in others," and the second is "When big brands make changes in how they do business, it affects everyone." Both speak to the fact that we live in a very connected world and libraries today are just as affected by trends in business and industry as they are by what happens in the nonprofit sector. This is why following trends in different sectors is just as important as identifying trends in the library arena. Consumers today do not differentiate between the products and services they get at the library and the products and services they get anywhere else, so libraries have to stop assuming that somehow they are exempt from consumer expectations. We cannot be "good enough." We need to be "the best."

• SUMMARY OF WHAT I LEARNED •

- A consumer trend is a new expression of what people need, want, or expect from the products and services that they use in their lives.
- Learning to identify consumer trends can help make sense of the deluge of information available in today's environment and can provide a framework by which to understand rapid change.
- The skills required to identify trends include curiosity and the ability to consider why something is happening, how events connect and interact, and what need is being fulfilled by the trend.
- What happens to consumers in one place affects their expectations in others.
- When big brands make changes in how they do business, it affects everyone.
- Market research looks at what has happened, whereas consumer trends are forward thinking about where things could go next.
- Trend spotting can be a low-cost tool for organizations.

• RESOURCES •

The Cool Hunter (Roaming the USA and the globe so you're in the know), www.thecoolhunter.net

Cool Hunting (Online publication), www.coolhunting.com

"Presentations," *The Irreverent Librarian* (blog), http://irreverentlibrarian.com/presentations

TrendHunter.com (World's largest community for trend spotting, cool hunting, and innovation), www.trendhunter.com

Trendwatching.com (Consumer trends and insights from around the world), http://trendwatching.com

"What's It Like Hunting for 'Cool'?," in *The Merchants of Cool: A Report on the Creators and Marketers of Popular Culture for*

Teenagers, Frontline/PBS, www.pbs.org/wgbh/pages/frontline/shows/cool/etc/hunting.html

• INTERVIEW QUESTIONS •

Why is it important to be aware of trends?

How can an organization tell when it is being successful with its trend tracking?

What skills does a trend spotter need to have?

Once a trend is identified that might be relevant to an organization, what kind of process does it need to have in place to take advantage of that trend?

What do you think is the difference between market research and trend tracking and why do you think a library would want to do one versus the other?

Do you think trend tracking can be done at a very local level or, by its very nature, only at the large, aggregate level?

Libraries do not tend to have a lot of extra money, people, or time to do trend tracking. What resources might they still tap in to? How would you suggest they screen for trends?

Libraries are going through a period of major change and evolution. How might trend tracking help them in that process?

A lot of trend tracking is in areas and industries that have no relationship to libraries. How might a library extrapolate learning from those trends that would be relevant to how it does business?

How would you respond to people who do not see the value in libraries doing trend tracking?

Have you seen any trends recently that might be particularly relevant to libraries?

One of the hardest parts of trend tracking is taking an idea that is very innovative and exciting and figuring out how to apply it in the library environment. What suggestions do you have that might help librarians do that more effectively?

What issues can come up during trend tracking?

Do you think it would be more helpful for libraries to look at individual examples of new trends and extrapolate ideas for libraries or to try to track broad conclusions that are more strategic and directional in nature?

"How will the underlying consumer expectations combine with local culture and values?" Can you talk more about this quote and how it might apply to libraries?

"With aspiration becoming increasingly globalized and age-agnostic, demographic segments are becoming less meaningful predictors of consumption patterns. If anything, four broad segments remain: tech vs. non-tech, rural vs. urban." Can you talk more about how this might apply to libraries?

Can you identify any nonprofits that you think do a great job of tracking and applying trends to their business?

8

LEARNING YOUR COMMUNITY

BRIAN KEVIN AND GINNY WRIGHT
Down East Magazine

• WHY THIS TOPIC •

Libraries in the past operated by opening their doors and welcoming all from the community who walked through those doors. Librarians did not have to think about how to increase the numbers of library users nor about how to increase circulation numbers. They simply needed to help the people who came to the library, and by doing that, the librarians reached most of the community.

Today, the world has changed. Libraries generally have to rationalize the financial support that they receive by demonstrating usage by their communities. Librarians are expected to provide services, not just in the library, but also out in the community. The concept of the embedded librarian who is providing library services out in the community is now becoming an accepted practice.

If libraries are going to provide new services successfully, they need to understand what type of services their communities want and the best ways to provide those services effectively. To do this, libraries need to learn more about their communities. Who are the people living in these communities? What new groups are moving into these communities and what is happening to the "old-timers"? What concerns do people have? What issues do people see developing in their own lives with which libraries could help them? As I started thinking about the businesses that I might talk to about this topic, I realized that what I really wanted to find was a business that could give libraries the skills to "interview" their communities. A reporter is probably the most informed person in town when it comes to who is doing what, the problems the community is facing, and the potential solutions that people in the community think are reasonable. Essentially, I wanted to find a newspaper reporter to see what libraries could learn from the newspaper industry. However, as in many small towns, our local newspaper no longer has the cadre of reporters that it once had in the past. Instead, I decided to seek out magazine writers because they share many of the same skills as newspaper reporters. They have to know how to find sources of information, how to talk to people, and how to boil down large ideas to a few key points. My search led me to *Down East* magazine.

• WHY THIS ORGANIZATION •

Down East magazine is a Maine institution. It was started in 1954 with the mission of "holding up a mirror to Maine" and has done that consistently since then. When people leave Maine to move somewhere else, reading *Down East* is one way they stay in touch with "home." For summer people, *Down East* is a way of keeping those spectacular Maine summer days fresh in their minds during the snows of winter. For people who are newly arrived in Maine, *Down East* is one way of starting to understand what makes Maine tick. I decided to talk to writers at *Down East* to see whether I could find transformative ideas about how libraries could discover more about their own communities. The *Down East* writers are connected with people across Maine, and they definitely have methodologies to help them learn about what is happening in the state. My goal in this discussion was to understand how they do their work and how librarians might learn from them.

• INSIGHTS FROM THIS INTERVIEW •

LEARNING

To know what is going on in a community and what people are thinking, you have to get out into that community and talk to those people. Both Ginny Wright and Brian Kevin from *Down East* magazine talked about how important it is to be in a community in order to understand that community. When you stay in the office, you start to lose the sense of what is on people's minds. You need to sit across from people and talk to them face-to-face to get the nuances of what they are saying. Keep in mind that this perspective comes from two writers who work for a magazine with an extraordinarily engaged readership. *Down East* has people who write letters, send e-mails, and submit pictures on a regular basis. Yet, despite this, both writers believed it was critical to be out talking to people directly.

▶ Implication

Librarians need to get out of their libraries and be in their communities. This seems very obvious, but I think librarians in particular forget this is true. We sit in our buildings and assume that the people who walk in our doors represent "the world." They do represent a part of the world but certainly not the whole thing. Even if your library does not plan to have librarians who are embedded in the community, the librarians still need to get out and talk to folks. If you are naturally outgoing, it is easy to go to the local coffee shop and strike up a conversation with folks there. However, this can be a difficult task for people who might be introverts, but there are ways to make it easier. Consider volunteering in the town where your library is located. Even a couple of hours a month out of the library will help you build a better understanding of how your community operates. Take your dog to the local dog park and chat with folks there. Listen to what folks are saying in the line at the grocery store. Chat with the server when you go out to dinner. Ask questions and then listen to the answers. A willingness to learn can help get you past a lot of the nerves involved in chatting with people whom you do not know.

▶ Idea

Offer your employees the opportunity, once a month, to go out into the community and listen in some capacity. Give them two to three hours of paid time to be out of the library doing something in the community that increases their exposure to how people think outside the library. They can volunteer to read books to seniors or go chat with people in the local coffee shop. It does not matter what they do, as long as it is in the community where the library is located and they are actively engaging in some capacity with the people who live in that community. The key to making this idea work is that when they come back, they need to write up a simple report (one page or less or, easier, a standardized format that everyone simply fills in) in which they share what they learned so that the information is captured for the entire library staff. You may want to make this community engagement an optional activity. You want only those people who are committed to it and understand its value to be the ones doing it. As these employees go out into the community and have successes in building relationships and learning more about the community, gradually other employees will become more interested in getting involved.

I can immediately hear all of the reasons why this will not work, and they are generally related to funding authorities or the board of trustees not understanding how librarians could possibly be working outside the library. My suggestion is that the library director should meet with these individuals, explain the concept, and define why it will be valuable to the library and the community. If board members are truly concerned, consider inviting them to go with employees to witness the process firsthand.

LEARNING

Newspapers are still a great way to understand what is happening in a local community, so do not forget to check local newspapers. During my conversation with Ginny, I discovered that she still considers local newspapers to be a great way of learning about a community. When she gets ready to do an article about a specific town in Maine, she told me she starts by doing background research that involves reading recent newspapers and making a stop at the local library. I pounced on that statement, of course, and asked how she uses the library. She looks at local town histories for context about how a town got to where it is today, and those local histories are generally found at the local library. I also found it interesting that she still considered newspapers to be a good resource, given that so many smaller papers have disappeared or now use primarily syndicated content. Her perspective was that even if they only come out once a week, they are still a great way of understanding what is happening in a town. Local newspapers are also a great resource because often they use local citizens as reporters and those people have a great understanding of who the players are in a town and what they are doing. If your library is in a college town (as is Brunswick, Maine, home of Bowdoin College), do not forget to provide access to the college's student newspapers also because they provide yet another perspective that might be missed by library employees.

► Implication

If library employees are not keeping up with the local newspapers, they are missing a great way to gain insight into their community. I think many people, including myself, have essentially written off newspapers as the way of collecting our day-to-day information. However, obviously this tool still exists and still has value when it comes to knowing what is going on in a community. Most libraries still provide access to newspapers, either in the traditional format or online. Apparently, librarians should be reading them too!

► Idea

Encourage library employees to read any local newspapers in your community by providing them with free access, either online or via hard copies in the staff room. In today's commuter age, it is often the case that library employees do not live in the towns in which they work. This can seriously curtail the ability of the employees to really understand the community they serve. Providing free access to local newspapers and making it easy for employees to read those papers by putting them in a staff room or giving everyone online access can help increase the employees' sense of connection with the people in their community.

LEARNING

Social media and blogs are rich sources of information about a community. Writers live for Twitter. "Ten Ways Twitter Is Valuable to Journalists," an article by Steve Buttry on *The Buttry Diary* blog, does a great job of identifying how Twitter can be used to collect information, amazingly quickly, about almost any topic (http://stevebuttry.wordpress.com/2012/08/27/10-ways-twitter-is-valuable-to-journalists). I recommend reading this article in conjunction with this chapter, particularly if you have never quite figured out what is so great about Twitter.

Blogs are another great way of collecting ideas. Of course, the caveat to this is that blogs generally have a bias of some sort and are certainly not neutral sources of information (which is true of most social media). However, they can provide yet another source of information about a community that can help round out your understanding of what makes the community the way it is.

▶ Implication

More and more community information is available online and via social media, providing rich resources for libraries seeking to learn about their communities. Facebook often has pages for local businesses, local community organizations, local businessmen, local celebrities, and local politicians. They use Facebook to share information and increase awareness about their activities. Like their pages and they become a source of tremendous information. The same is true for all of the social media options available today.

▶ Ideas

If you are not quite sure how to get started with blogs, do a Google search: blogs [name of your library's community and state]. In one search, I identified blogs for a local politician, the two local hospitals, two realtors, the historical society, a bank, and the town high school track and field team. Obviously, you are not going to read every one of these blogs every day. However, you can pick and choose several that you think will add to your knowledge base about the local community and follow them on a regular basis.

Consider recruiting a social media monitor from library staff. A social media monitor can have the responsibility of finding local Facebook pages, blogs, Pinterest pages, and so forth. The monitor will read those resources and make sure that other library employees understand what they tell the library about the community. The social media monitor could also develop a finding aid to local social media sites that, in turn, could be shared with library users who might be interested.

LEARNING

Ask everyone in the community with whom you speak to provide names of other people whom you can contact about the same topic. Reporters and writers use this tactic regularly. When you find one resource that informs what you are writing or trying to learn, it is a good bet that this resource will know of other people to contact about the same topic. It is also much more likely that people will be comfortable talking to you if you have been referred to them by your first contact. Again, you have to be aware of potential bias, but the trade-off is access to more ideas and information about the topic at hand.

▶ Implication

As you go into the community in your role as a library employee, ask the people you discover who have special insight or knowledge about your town if they can recommend other similar folks with whom you can chat. It can almost be guaranteed that one person who has a special knowledge base about your town will be able to point you to other folks with the same interests. For example, if you have trains running through your community, the odds are good that as you start to get to know more about your town, you will encounter a train enthusiast. This person will be able to tell you all about the history of the trains, what type of trains run now, who uses the trains, and whether or not people in town support the trains. Then they will give you the name of five other people in town who also love trains and can tell you a whole lot more about them. I think this is generally the case with enthusiasts of any topic; they always find one another so they can talk about their mutual enthusiasm. In any case, they can end up being a wonderful resource for those who are learning about their communities.

▶ Idea

Pick one topic (e.g., politics, the school system, ethnic groups, religious groups, lobstermen!) that you would like to learn more about in your community. Request help from fellow library employees to find one local expert on this topic. See if you can set up time to meet with that expert to tap their knowledge base, explaining that this is something you are doing as a library employee with the goal of learning more about your community. At the end of the conversation, ask whom else you might contact in town about the same topic. Once you have talked to several people, share what you have learned on your library's website and put up a Facebook post about it. Ask for input from those two places. By the end of this process, I am guessing that you will have collected enough information that you will now be considered an expert on the topic yourself!

LEARNING

Keep a list of your local contacts and make sure you stay in touch with them. Writers and reporters know this rule. Good contacts are worth maintaining because you can always go back to them for more information or they might provide a new twist that will lead to a new story. Staying in touch can be as simple as a quick e-mail with a link to something that you read online that made you think of that person. It can be taking the person out for a cup of coffee if you are in the area. Or it might mean passing on information that could be helpful to that person. The point is to maintain each relationship as part of a network of contacts.

▶ Implication

Developing and maintaining a network of contacts outside the library profession can help substantially expand the pool of support for your library. By expanding the list of whom we, as library employees, know in our communities and maintaining ongoing relationships with those people, we are developing a much broader base of support than we have today without those contacts. But contacts are not always people who go to the library or send the library money, so how are they helpful to the library? They are helpful because contacts can help you in many different ways besides sending money or going to the library. They can provide you with the names of people to help you with special projects. They can speak well of the library in the community in places where you do not have access. They can influence people with political clout who then can help get more funding for the library. Bottom line: you do not always immediately know how a contact can be helpful but it can never hurt to build connections.

I am not a good or natural networker. I get uncomfortable asking other people for help even when it is for the library. I like to help other people, but I do not like being in the position of having to ask for help. So, based on reading a lot about networking, I focus my networking on figuring out how I can help other people rather than ask for help myself. My assumption has always been that if I concentrate on helping other folks, when I need help, it will come. This makes the whole process of networking feel much less like using people and much more like developing real relationships. And that is what networking really should be. I still have a lot to learn about being a good networker, but it is an important skill because it expands the pool of whom you know, what you learn, and the help that you receive in your community. Libraries could vastly expand their support network just by having library employees who consciously develop and maintain contacts in the community.

▶ Idea

Ask library employees to read Dig Your Well Before You're Thirsty: The Only Networking Book You'll Ever Need, *by Harvey Mackay (Currency Books, 1999), and then have a team discussion about it.* This classic book about networking articulates a simple process for meeting and staying in touch with people that is easy to follow, even for the terminally shy.

LEARNING

Provide a way for people to contact you with information about what is happening in the community. Journalists make themselves available to people with information. They have sources throughout a community. Today's writers actively solicit information via social media. When they have a story to write, they will often put a request on Facebook or Twitter or their webpage for anyone who might provide background or information about that idea to contact them. Ginny and Kevin provided me with an example of this in *Down East* magazine. The magazine was planning a feature story about the *Uncle Henry's* publication, available in Maine. It is an extremely popular weekly print publication of classified ads. As they say, *Uncle Henry's* "provides most anything under the sun." Prior to writing the article, *Down East* asked its readers on Facebook, Twitter, and its webpage if any of them had stories about *Uncle Henry's* that they wanted to share with *Down East* readers. This happens regularly today via all of the different social media that are available.

▶ Implication

Libraries can use social media proactively to collect information about the community's perspective on any topic. Libraries are so used to being the ones to provide information that I do not think it crosses the minds of librarians that they could also use social media to ask questions and get information from the community. Doing so can serve the purpose not only of informing library employees, but also of providing a forum for discussion about community events and issues. If libraries choose to do this, they will need to moderate these forums to ensure that those who participate do not break all the rules of civil behavior. However, even in that scenario, I think library-led online discussions could be extremely informative and useful both to the community and to the library. Libraries have to stay neutral to make sure anyone who wants to participate can do so without feeling like the library is manipulating the discussion.

Libraries can use other tools besides social media to encourage community discussions. Curtis Memorial Library recently obtained a grant with the local historical society that allowed us to hire Story-Corps to visit Brunswick and do oral histories with people of French-Canadian descent in the community. Most of these individuals had friends or family who worked in the Brunswick mills in the 1940s, 1950s, and 1960s, and our hope was to preserve some of the mill history by talking to them. It was a wonderful opportunity to get people to share their personal histories and preserve them for their families. However, what was particularly interesting was the fact that the oral history process brought many people into the library who had never been there before. They shared stories that were a core part of Brunswick's history, and none of us had ever heard them before. The stories were so interesting and new to those of us who had not grown up in Brunswick that we shared all of them via the library's webpage and our Facebook page. The response was very strong on our webpage because people had seen the Facebook postings about the oral histories, listened to them on the webpage, and then discussed some of what they had heard. Everyone learned more about the community, and social media played a key role in making this happen.

> Idea

Post a question to your community on your library's social media outlets about something important happening in your community. For example, "What do you think about the new cross-walks in downtown? Do they really slow down traffic on Main Street?" Post your question and see what happens. The library can correct information that is wrong, but otherwise you are there as only an observer who is providing a forum for the community to talk.

LEARNING

Look at your peers to see how they operate and to get new ideas. Of interest to me was Ginny's comment when I asked her where she gets ideas for new ways of writing or connecting with stories. She said she looks at what other magazines are doing. If she sees a really interesting way of telling a story, she will pay attention to it and think about how she might do a story that way.

▶ Implication

Talk to other community organizations and nonprofits to find out what they do to learn about their communities. Most community organizations and nonprofits have a need to understand their communities, similar to that of libraries. How do they do this? What tools do they use and do they have ideas that libraries can use?

▶ Idea

Call the director of the senior center in your community (most towns and cities have one of these) to find out how he or she learns about the community. What tools does the director use and are any of them applicable to the library? Might the two organizations work together to do a better job of learning about their community? If you have a partner in this process, it might seem easier to do and less intimidating. Plus, you can check what you hear and see with each other to correlate perspectives.

LEARNING

Always be aware of what you see happening in your community. Scanning the environment is something that good reporters never stop doing. Both Brian and Ginny indicated that they do not consider their jobs to end when they walk out of the door of *Down East* magazine. They always have an eye open to information and ideas as they come in, and they are always thinking about what they see and hear. As Brian said, "Even when we are off, we are on." Brian talked about how much he loves to talk to people and have conversations about anything. He always has feelers out and is always thinking about the next story.

▶ Implication

Library employees will hear more and learn more if they are always open to input, even when they are off the job. I know some library employees who would strongly resist this idea. They want to leave their jobs on Friday, go home, and not think about the library again until Monday. I understand this perspective and am sympathetic to the fact that when those people started their careers in libraries, it was probably the standard. I do think that this will be the last generation of library workers who will have this luxury. In the future, I think library employees will have to (and hopefully want to!) think about their jobs and their communities all the time. As a profession, we will not discover the creativity and innovation that we need to evolve unless we are thinking about our jobs a lot more than just thirty-five to forty hours a week.

▶ Idea

Develop a way to capture during your nonwork hours what you see, hear, and learn about your community. This idea works differently for different people. I am a Mac user at home, so on my Mac I keep the app Notes. When I learn or hear something that I want to remember with respect to my job, I write it down in Notes. I do this so I will not forget ideas, but I also do it so I do not drive myself crazy trying to remember something that I will absolutely forget the second I stop saying, "Don't forget, don't forget." It makes the process of scanning and collecting ideas and information very simple and nonstressful when I do it during my off hours.

LEARNING

Put in time every morning collecting information about your beat. A beat is a reporter's area of focus. So, a reporter might write stories about crime or politics or business or be a community reporter who focuses on a geographic area. In any case, most reporters will spend time every day being, as Brian put it so perfectly, "a conscious consumer of the culture and landscape." He makes a routine out of consuming media and reads a whole list of blogs, newspapers, and social media pages. With everything he reads, he is asking himself, "Can I make a story out of something like this?"

▶ Implication

Librarians can use their mastery of information to develop a daily routine for consuming media about their local community. Take ten minutes every morning before you start work to read one local and one state newspaper. Read ten Twitter feeds from local community members or organizations. Call up a friend that you made in the town office and find out how that person is doing and what is going on around town. Read a blog about local politics. The important point is to have a regular routine that becomes part of how you operate.

▶ Idea

Read your own library's website to see if there is anything on there that you missed. Curtis Library has many activities held in our community meeting room that are sponsored and executed by the public. This is wonderful because it means the library gets used heavily by our community and there is a wide variety of things always going on in the library. However, it also means that I am not always aware of everything happening at the library. I have had people ask me about an event and I did not know the details. It would be easy enough to address such situations while also learning more about what is going on in my community just by reading the calendar of events at Curtis Library.

LEARNING

Consider providing opportunities for community members to take over one of your social media channels (or to start a new channel) as a way of bringing a community perspective to your social media for at least a short period of time. This is an idea that *Down East* is exploring. The magazine has asked its community of readers whether any photographers are interested in managing its Instagram social media for a weekend. As you might guess, the response was enthusiastic. The magazine will be trying this out once a month, but Brian said that the first trial of the idea went very well and proved to be a great way to bring a different perspective to the magazine.

▶ Implication

Social media was developed to build relationships, and libraries can open up their social media to their communities with the goal of developing new relationships with help from community members. I think this could be a transforming idea in how libraries operate in the digital environment. We never have enough resources to develop social media channels the way we would like. Why not develop one channel specifically with the goal of making it for the community and the library together? You might bring in new library users, you would open yourself up to perspectives from the community, and you might discover ideas for new services and products that the community would like the library to offer.

▶ Idea

Let go of control for a short designated period of time by asking your community to take over one of the library's social media channels. I would suggest having a community member run something fairly simple, like an Instagram account, where the primary responsibility is to provide photos. The library could set up some very simple rules (e.g., "The opportunity is available only to amateur [or professional] photographers and pictures have to be family friendly"). You can publicize the idea, and you can be sure that the person in charge for the weekend will be telling his or her friends and family about the job, so you will attract that audience, if no other.

• THE BIG IDEAS FROM THIS INTERVIEW •

I think the learning "Social media and blogs are rich sources of information about a community" could be a very powerful tool for libraries. Libraries have been so busy developing their own social media channels that I am not sure they have even begun to explore using social media to learn more about their communities. This is now on my to-do list!

The learning "Consider providing opportunities for community members to take over one of your social media channels (or to start a new channel) as a way of bringing a community perspective to your social media for at least a short period of time" has the potential to be a game-changing tool for libraries. Libraries do not give up control of content very happily. However, if there are areas of social media that your library is not using at all because it just does not have enough people resources to make it happen, why not try this idea and bring in volunteers to start developing a new channel? At worst, you will have a new communication resource for the library, and at best, you may find yourself with a new, easy way to communicate with your community.

The learning "Keep a list of your local contacts and make sure you stay in touch with them" may not be news to everyone in the library profession, but I am willing to bet that for those librarians who actually do this, it is transformational. Most of us assume that our contacts in the community will stay solid regardless of how often we are in touch. However, all contacts need to be maintained if they are to be useful. Imagine how much more you could know about your community if you simply touched base with your key community contacts once a month.

• SUMMARY OF WHAT I LEARNED •

- To know what is going on in a community and what people are thinking, you have to get out into that community and talk to those people.
- Newspapers are still a great way to understand what is happening in a local community, so do not forget to check local newspapers.
- Social media and blogs are rich sources of information about a community.

- Ask everyone in the community with whom you speak to provide names of other people whom you can contact about the same topic.
- Keep a list of your local contacts and make sure you stay in touch with them.
- Provide a way for people to contact you with information about what is happening in the community.
- Look at your peers to see how they operate and to get new ideas.
- Always be aware of what you see happening in your community.
- Put in time every morning collecting information about your beat.
- Consider providing opportunities for community members to take over one of your social media channels (or to start a new channel) as a way of bringing a community perspective to your social media for at least a short period of time.

• RESOURCES •

"10 Ways Twitter Is Valuable to Journalists," by Steve Buttry, *The Buttry Diary* (blog), August 27, 2012, http://stevebuttry .wordpress.com/2012/08/27/10-ways-twitter-is-valuable- to-journalists/

• INTERVIEW QUESTIONS •

Down East has covered the same state day in and day out and has done this since 1954. What do you do to keep the stories fresh and interesting for your readers?

How do you keep your finger on the pulse of what is happening at the local level in Maine? In other words, how do you determine where the stories are?

When you develop local connections, how do you maintain them?

Do you research Maine's communities as a part of developing a story? If so, how do you do the research?

Do you stick with the "tried and true" in terms of content or do you try out new ideas? How do you get those new ideas? Do they come from readers or are they something that the magazine staff develops?

What do you think is the most successful feature of *Down East* and why?

Does *Down East* use social media at all as a way to get a handle on local Maine culture? How are you using social media?

"The goal of *Down East* has always been to hold a mirror up to Maine." Libraries are also reflections of their communities. What do you think libraries could learn from *Down East* about understanding and reflecting their communities?

Library newsletters (both electronic and paper) are one of the key ways that libraries talk to their current users. Do you have any suggestions about how a library might change its newsletter to attract new readers?

Library websites seem to be heavy on the use of photography (versus video) to report on events at the library. However, it seems like videos are a better way to really talk to library users. Has *Down East* considered the difference between these two methods of sharing information and gone toward one or the other?

How is it working having local photographers take over the *Down East* Instagram account? Would you suggest it as a good idea?

9

CREATING A GREAT WORKPLACE

MEREDITH JONES
Maine Community Foundation

• WHY THIS TOPIC •

I love my job, and I love going to work. It has been this way for me ever since I started in my career as a librarian. However, I have also spent years of working in jobs and environments that I disliked, so I empathize with people who are not happy at work. My goal as a library director is to make Curtis Memorial Library an outstanding workplace for its employees. However, I have not found much literature in the library profession about how to develop an exceptional workplace, and finding transformational ideas about this topic can be difficult. Therefore, I thought it would be useful to explore what is involved in creating the type of environment where people want to be. I decided to contact a nonprofit organization in Maine about the topic versus talking to a for-profit business because of the outstanding reputation this particular nonprofit has with respect to its workplace environment.

• WHY THIS ORGANIZATION •

My desire to learn more about how to create a productive and enjoyable work environment led me to the Maine Community Foundation (MCF). MCF has a well-deserved reputation as a great place to work in the state of Maine. I have worked with their employees during my time as a library director in Maine, and I have always been impressed with their professionalism and real interest in the work of the nonprofits of Maine. In 2013, MCF was identified as one of the sixty best places to work in Maine by the Maine State Council of the Society for Human Resources Management. This recognition reaffirmed my belief that MCF is a good place to have a career. Thanks to the help of Liana Kingsbury, Senior Foundation Officer at MCF, I was able to spend time talking with Meredith Jones, Chief Executive Officer (CEO) of the Maine Community Foundation.

• INSIGHTS FROM THIS INTERVIEW •

LEARNING

Part of what makes a wonderful workplace is the sense that employees are involved in joyful work. At the beginning of my interview with Meredith, she mentioned that MCF is involved in "joyful work," and I asked her why she used that expression. She explained that in her mind MCF employees are lucky because they get to build relationships with donors and then help organizations throughout Maine by sharing those financial resources through grants made by MCF. To her this is joyful work (and I agree!), and Meredith has the great energy and enthusiasm that would be expected from the CEO of any organization. However, from working with other MCF employees, I know that this attitude is shared by other staff members and seems, in fact, to be pervasive in the organization. Meredith obviously understands that when leaders are open about enjoying what they do, they help set the tone and tenor of an organization in a positive way and to make employees feel like they are part of something important.

▶ Implication

If library leaders are open and expressive about their passion for what they do, they help establish a perception that employees of the organization are working for a special place. Everyone wants to be part of a wonderful work environment, but employees tend to forget or take for granted what makes an organization special after they have been there for a long time. It is good to be reminded on a regular basis about why people want to work in libraries. This type of expressiveness has to start at the top of the organization to embed it in the culture so that others in the library who feel the same way can express their feelings comfortably. It is difficult to be positive about your workplace if everyone there complains about the library—you feel like a fish trying to swim upstream. However, if you hear your library leader talk on a regular basis about the parts of the job that he or she loves, it becomes much easier for you to express your own happiness in your job. A library that has a leader who feels privileged to be in his or her job always seems to be much more likely to have a staff that feels the same way.

▶ Idea

Once a year, have your library's leadership (library director, assistant director, department managers) spend a day sharing with the entire staff and library community what they love about working at the library. This can take a lot of different directions. Each person could write an article for the library's newsletter about why he or she chose to work at this library and what gets him or her up every morning to go to work (besides a paycheck). A library director might write a personal note to all of the library's employees, saying thank you for the work that each person does and identifying why that work is so important in making the library such a great workplace. The board of directors of a library might write a letter to library employees, saying thank you and sharing with employees why the board members are willing to use their valuable spare time to support the library as volunteers. A library director could put up a large piece of paper somewhere in the library, ask people to write down why the library matters to the community, and then share their comments at an all-staff meeting. The goal of all of these exercises is to facilitate the expression of why the work of the library (and its employees) is important and wonderful and to create an environment of positive energy and contentment about working at the library.

LEARNING

Being customer focused as an organization helps everyone move in the same direction and helps create a collegial, supportive environment. An important part of creating a great workplace is to ensure that everyone understands what the organization is there to do. When the organization's customer is central, the guiding light for decisions becomes "What is right for our customer?" This simplifies the decision-making process in the organization, and when there is disagreement, it tends to make resolution easier because the correct answer to a disagreement is whatever makes things right or better for the customer (versus whatever decision makes things better for the other individuals in the disagreement). Being focused on the customer also helps people work together because there is no value in guarding ideas or trying to claim credit for oneself. The end goal is to create an environment that is customer-centric, and anything that contributes to this is a positive and anything held back from delivering it is a negative.

▶ Implication

Being customer-centric as a primary guiding value for a library can help develop a collegial workplace. Libraries have many different areas of functional expertise: reference, teen services, programming, fund-raising, and so on. Frequently, library employees are scattered throughout a library building, fitting into any available spaces. Libraries that are open for more than thirty-five hours a week generally have employees who work different shifts to cover all of those hours, meaning that some employees on an evening shift might never run into other employees who work in the morning. All of these factors facilitate the development of independent work units that do not always have the opportunity to be collegial with coworkers in the library. If this dynamic is changed and there is a reason for sharing information and ideas (because you cannot provide great customer service across the library if you do not), then collegiality will become a necessity versus a luxury. However, this perspective has to be driven by a library's leadership. Being customer-centric must be a core value for the library.

▶ Idea

Ask each library employee to be a library customer. If feasible, ask library employees to go to a nearby library to try out its services (if it is not possible to go physically to another library, this same exercise can be done by visiting another library's website). Ask them to answer for themselves the following questions:

- On a scale of 1–5 (1 = poor, 5 = outstanding), how would you rate the customer service that you encountered at this library?
- How did you feel about your interaction as a customer (e.g., satisfied, really happy, irritated, downright angry)?
- What do you think made you feel that way?
- What could the library have done differently in this interaction (better or worse)?
- Did you learn anything about being customer focused that you can take back to work at your library?

The goal in this scenario is to get library employees to step outside their normal role as the people who provide service and instead become the ones who are asking for service. There are no right or wrong answers in these interactions. The goal is to have employees carry their own feelings and the resulting expanded perspective into their customer interactions on the job. If they have more empathy, then hopefully they will be less interested in being "right" and more interested in finding the right answer for the customer.

LEARNING

Being willing to embrace change helps create an environment that is flexible and can evolve comfortably. This is yet another way in which leaders, modeling the behavior they want to see, can do so much to move an organization in a new direction. An organizational leader who is comfortable not always being in control of decision making and actually encourages the controlled chaos of change can do a great deal to establish these perspectives as cultural norms that everyone accepts.

Sometimes, part of creating this type of environment is a willingness on the part of leaders to say, "I haven't a clue" when they don't know an answer or "I'm sorry" when they do something that does not work. Several times in our conversation Meredith said, "I don't know" or asked me, "What do you think?" about a point that came up. I know that she was very comfortable not having answers to everything I was asking and that, in turn, made me more comfortable. At the same time, she was honestly interested in my perspective. Both of these methods of interacting were very helpful in making me feel like we were working together on a project, and that sense of collegiality was very obvious.

▶ Implication

Part of creating a culture that is flexible and welcoming is a willingness on the part of library leaders to work in a collegial versus top-down fashion. For many years, library leaders have been in the position of being the top-level decision makers in their organizations. They are responsible for a small to midsize "business," they make hiring and firing decisions, and they are the court of last recourse for conflicts. I think one of the best signals that things are changing in a library in a positive way is a library director who is willing to be more collegial in his or her work process. When I hear someone say, "I don't know. What do you think?" I feel like we are working together on a problem rather than one or the other of us being expected to find all of the answers. When someone tells me that he or she was wrong about a decision, again, this makes me feel like we are working as equals versus in a manager-subordinate relationship. Being coworkers with others in your organization does a lot to develop the perspective that "we are all in this together," and that is a powerful way of creating a sense of team in a library.

▶ Idea

When a coworker confronts you in the workplace, defuse the situation through acknowledgment, apology, and invitation. For example, if someone comes rolling into your workspace, complaining about something that you have done incorrectly, look that person straight in the eye and say the following three things:

1. You are right.
2. I apologize.
3. What do you think I should do to address this situation?

(If you are a library director, try this exercise. If you are not a library director but would like to get your library director to do this, model the behavior yourself to see if you can "manage up.") By using this process, you are taking all of the wind out of the person who has the issue because you have agreed that he or she is correct and you have apologized for the issue. What else can this person say at that point? Your third comment then gets to the most important part of the discussion—what can be done to fix the situation—and you have invited him or her to work with you on finding an answer. That is what really matters.

One of the employees at my library tried this exercise with me once, and it stopped me dead in my tracks and really got me to consider what I was saying to him. I have used the idea myself since then and find it is a wonderful way to change the dynamic of a discussion from potentially contentious to collegial and open. If you are the library director, using this process demonstrates that you know you are not infallible, that you are willing to acknowledge your mistakes, and that you would like the help of your employee, working with you, to address those mistakes. If you are an employee speaking to a manager, this process is a way to demonstrate to your manager (in a completely acceptable fashion) a positive behavior that he or she would do well to mirror.

The other behavior that I think every library director should learn, if he or she does not already know it, is using the simple statement "I apologize." Directors are like everyone else. They have good days and bad days. On good days they can be inspirational leaders, and on bad days they can do really stupid stuff. If you can learn how to apologize when you do the stupid stuff, this will make a world of difference in helping people enjoy their workplace and feel like what they do is appreciated.

LEARNING

Organizational cultures do not always fit all employees, but the people who work in the organization need to support that culture even if they do not embrace it. When you are developing an organization that is fluid, embraces change, and is comfortable with ambiguity, the result may be a place that does not work for all of the organization's current employees. This is okay. One size does not fit all. However, at that point, employees who are not fitting in have two choices. They can figure out how they can support the culture even if they do not want to embrace it, or they can leave the organization. What they cannot do is stay and complain. A great workplace is dependent on having employees who want to be doing what they are doing.

▶ Implication

A well-balanced and harmonious work environment can be supported by clear communication to library employees about what the library's culture is, how library employees are expected to function within that culture, and the potential ramifications of not being willing to work within the culture. Yes, it can be very difficult to articulate the specifics of a library's culture. However, even an attempt at such would be very helpful in making expectations clear and consistent with respect to how the library runs. This, in turn, helps reduce anxiety and should help in getting everyone to move in the same direction.

▶ Idea

Develop a document that explains the library's culture to new library employees. Ask current employees to put together an "Our Culture" document to make sure it accurately reflects how they see the culture (and the library's leaders can learn a lot from the end result). What should you include in this document?

- Present the library's mission, vision, and values statements first because these are the guiding strategic elements of the library.

- Follow these with the library director's vision of the library's culture. This should not be a heavy strategic statement but more of a "just between us" statement that employees can understand quickly. For example, when I first started working at my library, I always said that I saw the library as an elephant (my favorite animal!) because the library is smart and valued by the community as being unique and special but also because anything that happens there does so slowly and deliberately. My vision was to teach that elephant to dance! I still wanted an elephant, but I wanted to teach it to move more quickly and to be more nimble.

- Include also the "rites and rituals" of the library. These would be any activities that are oriented to the library employees and meant to make them feel like they are part of something bigger than themselves. Examples might include yearly charity activities like collecting food for the homeless, holiday employee parties, participation in employee wellness events, and monthly celebrations of birthdays. This section should also indicate who plans these events and how and how new employees can get involved.

- Identify workplace norms. These include standards of dress and language (e.g., How do children address librarians? How should telephones be answered?) as well as small things like how name tags are worn, where employees park, and where employees eat.

- Explain rules of communication. In this section, you could briefly identify how the library shares information. Do you have a staff intranet? Do you write down issues or opportunities in a shared staff location? Do employees e-mail one another, talk on the phone, or talk in person most often? Do staff members socialize in groups together, and, if so, when and how can a new employee get involved?

▨ Include organizational stories and mythology, for example: When was your library founded and by whom? If there are additions to the original library building, when and how did they get funded and built? Are there any donors to the library whom everyone should know about (you do not want to be the new employee who meets a major donor and does not treat that person appropriately)?

None of this information needs to be extensive, and probably much of it already exists in other documents. Your goal in developing this document is to make it as short as possible and to use pictures and any other visual support element to help make it fun and easy to use. When you hand this to a new employee (and hopefully spend some time talking about it), you are in essence saying, "Join our group." This is what every new employee wants to hear.

LEARNING

A supportive workplace provides many avenues to share concerns and invites discussion with no negative ramifications. At MCF, Meredith meets with her employees every two weeks. This gives her a chance to check in with them, ask questions, ask for their help and advice if she needs it, and provide an opportunity for the employees to get her input. This helps ensure that everyone is moving in the same direction and that if she sees any potential issues, she can call them out before they get too big. She also mentioned that she regularly invites employees to discuss important issues in the organization and that their perspective, whether acted on or not, is highly valued. A staff retreat is held to give employees the opportunity to weigh in on strategic issues. Although she did not explicitly say it, I am guessing that Meredith also has an open-door policy. So, there are many opportunities for MCF employees to discuss issues affecting them, MCF, and MCF's donors.

▶ Implication

Library employees are more likely to feel like they are a valued part of an organization if they are given the opportunity to express their opinions and they understand how those opinions will be used. I have many times heard organizational leaders talk about the value of giving employees the opportunity to tell you what they are thinking. However, I think what makes this work (as in the case of MCF) is when the employees also understand how their opinions will be used by the organization. Sometimes organizations change what they are going to do because of what employees say. Sometimes they do not. If employees think that their ideas will be implemented but they are not, sharing can become a point of frustration and irritation versus a way of making a better workplace. By asking for input and telling employees how that input will be used, libraries can get the benefit of hearing from their employees without making them feel that what they are saying is being ignored.

▶ Idea

Develop a tracking sheet and call it something like "When you spoke, we listened." Identify employee ideas that have been raised in one column and in a second column identify what happened as a result of those employee suggestions. Provide a third column for further input from employees. Put this sheet in a place where employees can easily see it and keep it updated. Encourage employees to put in questions or concerns. Discuss the sheet at staff meetings. The goal of this idea is to demonstrate that the library's leaders are listening when ideas are identified and they are responding, sometimes positively and sometimes negatively, but always responding.

LEARNING

Doing the work of the organization in cross-functional teams helps break down barriers within the organization. This is a very logical concept. If you put together people from across an organization into teams, they will have to figure out how to work together to accomplish a common goal, they will learn to respect the skills that people in other departments bring to the table, and they will learn to solicit and listen to input from people who do work different from their own. Cross-functional teams are also great because, more often than not, they are also comprised of people from many different levels in an organization. This forces interactions between senior, mid-level, and junior employees that might never happen otherwise and helps create the sense of teamwork and belonging that can do so much to create a positive workplace.

▶ Implication

Cross-functional teams that are self-directed can accomplish tremendous work for an organization and provide a process for staff members to interact and learn from one another. Librarians tend to work side by side versus in teams. Learning to work in a team environment can be difficult. However, working this way does so much to help create a positive work environment that I encourage all libraries to try this if they have not already. Teams are most productive when they are self-directed, meaning the library director does not run the team. A group of coworkers will form (the team is developed), storm (conflict arises as team members get used to one another's styles), norm (balance ensues as they learn to work together), and perform (the team delivers on its mission)—the traditional four stages of team development—on their own much more quickly and effectively when they have the responsibility to make this happen versus assuming the director will be responsible.

Let me share an example at my own library. After I had been at Curtis Library for five or six years, one day I walked in and saw a group meeting in the conference room. Afraid that I had forgotten a meeting, I rushed in and apologized for missing the meeting. Everyone in the meeting very nicely and politely let me know that I was not supposed to be at the meeting and everything was fine. A group of senior managers had decided to meet together to address a large number of building and facilities issues that had cropped up recently. They were perfectly comfortable forming the group and deciding what issues needed to be addressed. Their plan was to develop recommendations about how to address these issues and then come to me with their recommendations. They saw a need in the library and proactively decided to address that need.

I went through several fairly interesting responses in my head in about a three-second period. First, I got defensive: they were doing *my* job! Once that went through my brain and I recognized it for being the stupid response that it was, my second thought was, "OMG! I'm so excited that these people feel empowered enough and have enough ownership of this organization that they will take the time to get together, form a team, and start doing this work! This is the most amazing group of library employees in the world without a doubt."

Since that time, this particular self-directed team has taken on two of the most challenging, intriguing, and cutting-edge projects that Curtis Library has had. I am brought in at the appropriate times to provide input and ideas and to find the money to make projects happen. However, they drive the agenda and I am thrilled that they do it. There is so much value in having cross-functional, self-directed teams that I think it is worth the effort to figure out how to make this happen at every library.

▶ Idea

Start small by putting together a self-directed team to work on a small project. Identify something that needs to happen in your library that is large enough to have an impact but small enough that you do not have to get every person in the library involved in the process. Make sure it is a project that can be successfully executed within a reasonable period of time. Find three to five people from different departments and different levels in the library who are already sold on the idea of self-directed teams and ask them to participate. If you are not a library leader, get your manager on board to ensure that you have the support that you will need from senior management to make this idea happen. Once completed, use this project as a case study to prove to your library's leadership why self-directed teams are a great idea and how they can contribute to the library's success. Then, keep using them!

LEARNING

Fairness does not necessarily mean treating everyone the same, but it does mean treating everyone with respect, assuming that they can act like adults, and giving them what they need according to their unique situations. Fairness is always a difficult conversation for leaders to have with their employees. Everyone has a different view of what is and is not fair, and often managers "step in it" because they think their actions are fair but their employees do not agree. Since MCF is such a role model for being a good workplace, I asked Meredith to talk a bit about this topic. Her perspective was interesting. She said that fairness does not necessarily mean that everyone is treated equally. She believes fairness is being treated with respect and as an adult, meaning that there is an expectation that rules do not need to be developed for every aspect of the workplace because adults know what is and is not appropriate. In her mind, fairness also means being as flexible and accommodating to the needs of individuals as possible.

▶ Implication

All library employees do not have to be treated exactly the same to ensure a fair organization. Instead, an organization can be perceived as being fair if all employees understand that everyone has the same opportunity to have their needs addressed on an individual basis and if there is a great deal of transparency around this practice.

For example, I am Mary's manager and she tells me she needs to leave ten minutes early every day to pick up her daughter. I tell her that this is okay but that she needs to make up the time by coming in ten minutes early every morning. I share this information with my staff and also tell them that if they have issues like this, I am happy to work with them. John then asks if he can come in half an hour early every day and leave half an hour early because that would reduce the time of his commute by forty-five minutes due to traffic flow. I tell him yes and, again, share this information with the team. Mary and John have been treated differently, so they could potentially say I am not being fair because I am not treating them in exactly the same way. However, what I am doing is providing both of them with the same access to flexibility and adjusting that flexibility based on their unique needs, which is fair. I am also sharing this information with the rest of my staff to ensure that they understand they also have access to flexibility with respect to timing as long as they are able to make up lost time.

This is a different approach to fairness from much of what I have learned about being a manager, that to be fair you have to treat everyone exactly the same. I like the flexible perspective better because it provides more opportunity for managers to address the individual needs of employees. However, I also think that this approach most likely requires the skills of an experienced manager to apply it smoothly and appropriately.

▶ Idea

If fairness has become an issue at your library, consider holding moderated small-group discussions about the topic. Mix employees together from different levels and functions of the library. Discuss the difference between being treated fairly and being treated equally. Are they the same in employees' minds or are they different? What do library employees want when they say they want fairness? Do they want to be treated exactly the same, regardless of their needs or do they accept that they can be treated differently but fairly? To facilitate the discussion, try the fairness exercise called the Ultimatum Game. Tell two individuals that they have a pot of money to share between them. One person is responsible for suggesting how to divide the money. The other person has to agree or disagree with that proposal. If he or she disagrees with the proposal, then no one gets any money. After the exercise is over, discuss how the two players felt and how their perspectives about fairness affected their decisions about the money. There are no right or wrong answers when having discussions like this. The goal instead is to air a topic that has become contentious and give people the opportunity to expand their understanding of what fairness means to them and to the people with whom they work.

LEARNING

Trust is all about believing that you are getting good, timely information. My conversation with Meredith about fairness led into a discussion about trust. How do you build trust in a workplace so that people feel comfortable when issues arise or change happens? Meredith's perspective is that people feel trust in their workplace when they feel like they know what is happening. So, taking this a step further, to be a trusted employer, you need to ensure that you do an outstanding job of communicating with your employees on a regular basis. One of the problems with this statement is that "on a regular basis" might be daily for one employee and monthly for another employee. So, an important part of the process of communication is to define when it will happen and under what circumstances (e.g., in meetings, online, verbally).

► Implication

Developing strong channels of communication is critical to ensuring that everyone in an organization feels appropriately informed. Libraries are difficult organizations in which to develop strong lines of communication. Some employees are full-time and some part-time. People work different shifts, different days, in different departments, and on different floors. Some staff eat lunch at their desks, whereas others use the staff room. Some read e-mails religiously, others communicate in person, and still others will take the time to read the library's intranet. To reach all of these people requires ingenuity, flexibility, and creativity. I have personally discovered that no matter how often or how much I share information, invariably, one library employee will turn to me and say, "I didn't know that! Why didn't you share that?" Argh!

I stopped trying to share information across every possible channel of communication in the library. I invariably missed a channel, and in the process of trying to offer information in so many places, I would start to get confused, cross-post, share the same information twice, or not share it at all. I now have three goals for sharing information across the entire library: (1) Share the information in writing on the library's intranet. It is the employees' responsibility to check the intranet every day, and it is my responsibility to put information on it. (2) Share information verbally at all-staff meetings. Some employees just want to hear information from a person rather than read it. By communicating at staff meetings and in writing, my hope is that I will be hitting both the visual and verbal learners. (3) I share more rather than less, and I share with more people rather than fewer people. I used to assume that I could figure out who should know what information. I have discovered that I never get it right. So, rather than pick and choose and invariably be wrong, I work on the assumption that it is never bad to have more people know more information. I am a big advocate of a transparent organization, so this perspective has worked for me.

▶ Idea

Ask library employees to fill out a survey about communications. Ask about *how* information is conveyed and *what* information is conveyed. Is there a method of communication that might be more effective than what is used today? Do employees feel like they know the right information at the right times? It is so helpful to hear from employees about what is and is not working. They are obviously the best ones to tell you when you are communicating in a way that works for them.

LEARNING

A great work environment establishes a common, shared mission but provides the latitude for people to achieve that mission in their own way. Put another way, a good workplace lets people work in the way that is most effective for them versus trying to push the square peg into the round hole. Meredith talked about the fact that there are two MCF offices, one in Ellsworth, Maine, and one in Portland, Maine. The offices have different cultures, based on what works for the employees who use each office. However, what unites the two offices is the organization's mission, so the small differences in culture do not matter. Flexibility seems to be the key in allowing MCF to pursue its goals with single-minded focus but at the same time create a work environment that is fluid enough to meet the unique needs of different people.

▶ Implication

Focus about what, flexible about how. Libraries have an opportunity to improve their workplace in a fairly simple way. Most of us cannot dramatically increase employees' wages. However, we can increase the flexibility regarding how library employees work, providing them with the opportunity to do work in the way that works best for them. If one employee wants an afternoon at home once a week to get organized for the next week, is that really such a difficult thing to provide? If another employee works best in a quiet environment and cannot get enough done in a shared staff space, think about how this need might be met. Go back to the previous discussion about the difference between fair and equal. Not everyone has to be treated exactly the same in order to be treated fairly.

▶ Idea

Ask library employees to talk with their managers about what type of work environment is most productive for them. Brainstorm with library managers about how the library might provide those types of workspaces.

LEARNING

Hire for fit and attitude, train for skills, and expect everyone to be an "A" employee. Meredith has the perspective that organizational fit and attitude are more than 50 percent of what is important when hiring. She needs people who can fit into the existing culture because this allows for greater effectiveness and efficiency in those individuals' work right from the beginning. And if you have someone with the right attitude (proactive, interested in learning, full of passion about the job), you can train him or her to have the skills that you want. She added that she expects every employee to be an "A" employee, meaning a top performer. When interviewing, she considers the interviewees' listening skills, what they might add to the organization, and what they might add to the management team. She does not reward employees for exceptional performance because that is what is anticipated from all employees when they are hired and because she does not know of a fair way to quantify someone's accomplishments that are above the norm. However, salaries at MCF are at 60 percent of market average at midpoint to address the fact that employees are expected to be top performers from day one.

▶ Implication

Hiring new employees is one of the most important jobs in a library and should be the top priority for all involved staff members when the opportunity arises. You cannot build a great workplace if you are not focused carefully on hiring the right people for both a job and the organization. You need to understand what "fit" means in your library and then hire people who will be able to meld into that environment, or if you are trying to change the library's culture, hire people who can redefine the fit for the library. I am of the opinion that the library director should be involved in some capacity in every hiring decision in the library because the director is the person responsible for defining organizational culture. I also think the library director needs to be involved in hiring on a very hands-on level because he or she needs to drive the agenda to hire only the best employees. Everyone gets tired during a long interview process, and it is very easy to pick a candidate because everyone is just worn out and wants to get it over with. It is the director's responsibility to make sure that if a candidate is not top quality for some reason, the search continues.

▶ Idea

Ask the library director to write a statement defining "the ideal person for this job" for each new hire at the library. This is not a job description. Instead, it is meant to be a subjective description of what the best possible candidate might look like for a specific job. It sets the bar for the type of candidate that the director wants to hire and clearly defines expectations about what a top candidate is. Obviously, no one is going to be a perfect hire. However, by establishing ahead of time what you hope to find, you are making it harder to settle for a "B" candidate when you want an "A+" candidate!

The following is an example of what this ideal person statement might look like if written to hire an employee who will be both an administrative assistant and a building manager:

> The best possible new hire for this job would be someone who has exceptional customer service skills, a very pleasant, calm personality that can address building emergencies quietly and calmly, and a genuine interest in making sure that the library is an outstanding community institution. Not much can upset this person. This person is comfortable walking a drunk patron out of the building without making that person angry and can also efficiently get workmen into the building to fix a flood in the basement. This person can work equally comfortably on his or her own or on a team. This person is equally comfortable working on the computer as working on a leaky faucet. He or she can manage the ins and outs of the library's administrative work efficiently and effectively and is willing to do whatever it takes to get the job done. This person has a sense of humor; enjoys the quirkiness of library patrons, volunteers, and staff; and generally is upbeat. This person assumes the best of coworkers but when there are issues is willing and able to address those issues head-on in a constructive manner.

The ideal candidate summary is not meant to establish impossible expectations but rather to clarify for everyone involved in hiring new employees what the expectations are as to the level at which that employee will operate.

• THE BIG IDEAS FROM THIS INTERVIEW •

I think the big idea from this discussion that has the potential to change how libraries operate is "Trust is all about believing that you are getting good, timely information." I personally never thought about trust in the context of communication and information, but when it came up in this conversation, it made total sense to me. If you feel like you know what is happening in your workplace and why, then you are much more likely to vest your trust in the people running the organization than if you think your information is not accurate or timely. I have read in multiple places that organizational leaders generally communicate as much as ten times less than they need to in order to develop trust among their employees. This seems like a big opportunity for libraries to increase the level of trust across their organizations.

• SUMMARY OF WHAT I LEARNED •

- Part of what makes a wonderful workplace is the sense that employees are involved in joyful work.
- Being customer-focused as an organization helps everyone move in the same direction and helps create a collegial, supportive environment.
- Being willing to embrace change helps create an environment that is flexible and can evolve comfortably.
- Organizational cultures do not always fit all employees, but the people who work in the organization need to support that culture even if they do not embrace it.
- A supportive workplace provides many avenues to share concerns and invites discussion with no negative ramifications.
- Doing the work of the organization in cross-functional teams helps break down barriers within the organization.
- Fairness does not necessarily mean treating everyone the same, but it does mean treating everyone with respect, assuming that they can act like adults, and giving them what they need according to their unique situations.
- Trust is all about believing that you are getting good, timely information.
- A great work environment establishes a common, shared mission but provides the latitude for people to achieve that mission in their own way.

▪ Hire for fit and attitude, train for skills, and expect everyone to be an "A" employee.

• RESOURCE •

The Great Workplace: How to Build It, How to Keep It, and Why It Matters, by Michael Burchell and Jennifer Robin (Jossey-Bass, 2011)

• INTERVIEW QUESTIONS •

Maine Community Foundation has been identified as one of the "best places in Maine to work." Can we start by talking about why you think the organization has been ranked as such?

One of the key elements that are identified as being important in developing a great workplace is that the employees *trust* the people they work for. As a senior manager, what do you do think managers need to do to inspire trust?

People frequently define a great workplace as one that respects its employees. How do you think an organization can effectively demonstrate respect for its employees?

When people talk about wanting to be treated fairly at their job, what do you think they mean?

Communication flow is obviously an important part of a great workplace. How does MCF facilitate the flow of information across the organization?

Do you think it is important to have a unifying workplace culture? How can you develop that without making people feel like their individual differences are not important and not valued?

How do you develop a culture in an organization filled with very strong individuals who may resist or resent the idea of needing to "fit in"?

Google hosts a weekly town hall meeting known as TGIF. Employees from anywhere in the world can submit questions for the speakers to address. Does MCF do anything similar to that and, if so, how does it work? Do you think technology could do the same thing (using an internal network platform like SharePoint) or do you see value in the human interaction?

Not having "stupid rules" has also been identified as another indicator of a good workplace. What do you think constitutes "stupid rules"?

If a good workplace includes leaders who are far-sighted, passionate, courageous, wise, generous, and trustworthy, how do you build those traits in your leadership?

How are people encouraged and good work acknowledged and rewarded at MCF? How often does this happen?

One of the indicators of a healthy work environment is one in which people engage in conflict productively versus avoiding it. What is your perspective about this? How is conflict addressed at MCF? Does MCF train people about managing conflict with coworkers?

What ideas might you suggest as to how library leaders (who tend to stay in their jobs for many years) can refresh their thinking and leadership skills on a regular basis to ensure that they stay focused on having a great work environment?

What do you think are the biggest obstacles to creating a great workplace environment?

If you were a library leader, what would you do to make sure your library was a great workplace?

10

CONTENT CURATION

LIZ DOUCETT
Curtis Memorial Library

• WHY THIS TOPIC •

Think about what a museum curator does. He or she collects art related to a specific topic (one artist, a school of artists, a period in an artist's career) and adds value to the museum visitor by defining the link or connection between the various pieces and by providing commentary, making it easier to understand the exhibit as a whole. Today, individuals and companies are curating collections of articles, blogs, photos, art, information, ideas, and designs based on their interests or business. Then, they are providing an overview or commentary or defining the relationship among the pieces being curated. These "shows" are then shared with the public. Companies assume that through content curation they will be building relationships with people who value the content. They expect and hope that these relationships will result in people bringing their business to these companies with whom they have now developed a relationship.

Libraries already provide a variation of content curation. If you walk in the door of many libraries today, you will find books in displays with some sort of common theme. For example, you might find a display of "If you like Stephen King, try these" or "For the lover of vampire romance." Putting books together under a theme is a wonderful way of capturing the attention of book browsers in the library and of getting readers to try new authors and topics. Librarians add value by knowing what books or authors can be related to one another through genre, theme, or content. Content curation is a concept that libraries understand and do well.

Content curation today is most often a digital experience. It is a role tailor-made for the libraries of the future because it will take so little to move from brick-and-mortar content curation to the digital version. Libraries can do content curation in different ways, all of which will add value for the library user. They can promote local content creation by authors, artists, and photographers. They can share their already existing expertise by curating content online around topics like literacy or genealogy or local history. They can develop expertise around new topics like financial literacy or community engagement and curate content relating to those topics. Content curation is a compelling way for libraries to establish relationships with new elements within their communities and to enhance what they are providing to their communities as a whole. It is a topic well worth exploring.

I must also add a quick caveat on what content curation is *not* in my definition. Content curation is not setting up your website to automatically share information from your blog on Twitter or Facebook. This is a delivery mechanism from one location to another and provides little added value (other than making your life a bit simpler). When you think of content curation, think about the added value provided either through the unexpected combination of different content or through commentary or through just the choice of materials. These are what makes content curation particularly valuable.

As part of this book, I had hoped to interview a company that was involved in content curation but was unable to find one. I decided to go ahead and do the research on the topic myself and develop a chapter based on that research because this is a potentially transforming concept for libraries to understand and apply to their work. Please note that my format for this chapter is slightly different from that for the other chapters in this book. Because I was doing the research versus interviewing someone whose perspective I needed to interpret, I incorporated implications for libraries directly into each Learning section.

• INSIGHTS FROM THE RESEARCH •

LEARNING

Content curation is useful to libraries because it can help them build relationships with new audiences in their communities. When a library decides to become a content curator, there are many ways that this can be accomplished. A library might decide to curate content about the local arts community. The library might provide regular curated content about the newest consumer technologies with the goal of attracting seniors who want to learn more about technology. Information about financial literacy can be shared with the goal of attracting young adults, newly out of college, who are facing the need to learn to manage their own financial health. Whatever the focus of the curated content, the benefit of doing this for the library is the opportunity to develop a reputation as a knowledgeable source that provides valuable information to an audience on a topic of particular interest. Over time, the goal is that by curating content that people want to receive, the library will develop an ongoing relationship with that audience that will translate into use and support of the library.

As you consider the idea of providing curated content, keep in mind that it can expand beyond just written content. Curation can cover almost anything, including topics like art, music, design, local politics, and local business. If you can find the content and you think there is an audience for it, you can put yourself in the business of content curation.

▶ Idea

Browse the sites of companies/organizations that are doing content curation to get an understanding of what some of the different permutations of curation can look like. Here are some examples to get you going:

- The social media site Pinterest is all curated content. Check out the Whole Foods Market Pinterest page (www.pinterest.com/wholefoods) with content focused on healthy living.
- PepsiPulse (www.pepsi.com/en-us/d) provides content curation around anything having to do with pop culture.
- The United Nations provides content curation about current events through its Storify account (https://storify.com/un) with the goal of getting out correct content about world events.
- The Book Cover Archive offers "An Archive of Book Cover Designs and Designers" (http://bookcoverarchive.com) "for the purpose of appreciation and categorization."
- Lion Brand Yarns has developed a video library (www.lion brand.com/video) that provides content in the form of videos to enhance the skills of knitters and people who crochet.

LEARNING

Before you start curating content, identify the audience that you want to reach and why you want to reach that audience. It is easy to get completely overcome by the process of curating content. There is so much content available today that you may feel like giving up before you even get started. To avoid this, it is helpful to identify whom you are trying to reach with your content curation and why you want to reach them. Are you hoping to attract new library users? Do you want to provide a service to part of the community that already uses the library, such as young parents? Do you want to attract new online library users—those folks who do not walk into the library very often but will be happy to use its digital resources once they learn about them? Is your content targeted to seniors who want to learn more about computer skills?

Once you identify the audience that you want to curate for, identify your goal in doing this. What action do you want these people to take as a result of your content curation? Are you trying to attract them to the brick-and-mortar library? Do you want them to use a new service that is available online? Are you trying to develop a relationship with a new potential library constituent by sharing wonderful content? Again, the more carefully you think about what you want to happen as a result of your content curation, the more it will help you define the content that you need to provide.

▶ Idea

Brainstorm to develop a persona for each audience that you want to reach with content curation. A persona is a detailed description of an audience, using one person (the persona) as a stand-in for the entire audience. Your goal in developing a persona is to understand as much as you can about the needs that this audience has and how your content curation can help address those needs. The information that you want to consider will include identifying the demographics of audience members, their behavior, any facts that you might have about them, and, finally, the needs that they have in their lives. Marketers will do this in great detail, but libraries can also do it, based on what they know about their communities and what they can research easily. This should not take up huge amounts of time. A persona might also describe a "day in the life" of an audience member and/or the steps that the audience member will take to become involved with a product or service. Developing a persona is simply an easy way to help you think carefully about the audience that you want to reach through your content curation.

The following is an example of a persona that describes a young adult audience that a library would like to get more involved in using library services online:

> Hannah Hipster is a twenty-six-year-old woman who went to Bowdoin College and got a degree in studio art. She is an oil painter and does landscapes in a contemporary style. She is single and lives on her own. She is still located in Brunswick, Maine, in an apartment with two room-mates, and works at the local community college as a receptionist as she tries to get a job working in an art gallery in Portland. She does not make much money and saves her funds carefully to purchase art supplies, to go to museums, and to attend art openings. Hannah loves indie

movies and loves going to the movies but only has time to do that on weekends. She would be perfectly happy if she could watch an indie movie every night of the week. That is what she and her community of friends talk about when they get together, and the more Hannah knows about the latest movies, the more "cred" she gets with her friends about being in the know. Hannah has not gone to a public library in years because she now gets everything she wants in terms of reading online. However, if she knew that the library provided free access to IndieFlix, she would jump at the chance to use the service. Hannah uses Facebook and Twitter (but does not follow the local library's pages), and she still reads the Bowdoin student newspaper online. The goal of content curation for this persona is to raise awareness among young adults recently graduated from college and living in the Brunswick area about the digital services provided for free to local residents, particularly focusing on access to IndieFlix. The content curation process will focus on curating a page on the local library's website, updated two to three times a week, identifying great indie movie content. The content might include lists like "Best Young Independent Filmmakers" or "Best 2014 Indie Flix from the Top Three Film Festivals," reviews of new movies by staff members, or content from the movie industry newspapers.

Having a clear persona for each audience that your library wants to attract will help ensure that the library will have a clear strategy for development of content curation. If you would like to see examples of more personae, Google "persona" and click on "Images." The results will give you a good sense of the degree of detail that can be included for a persona and how organizations use them to curate content.

LEARNING

Identify the topics for content curation about which your library can become a sought-out source of information in the community. Spend the time to determine the topics about which your library could very quickly become a thought leader, as compared to topics in areas where the library would have to teach itself before it could start teaching others (see the following Idea section). One of the side benefits of becoming a content curator is that, in addition to providing rich resources for your community and raising awareness about the library's resources, your library can also become known as a thought leader on specific topics. This means that people will start to refer to the library as "the expert about XYZ." That, in turn, will cause members of the community to start coming to the library for information "from the experts," thus building awareness about the library and the services that it provides. However, you do not want to put your library out there as a thought leader until you are ready to act in that capacity, so do the research before you start curating. Keep in mind that library employees have personal hobbies that may help with this project. If you already have a movie lover on staff, why not ask that person to become a content curator around this topic? This will benefit the community and the library and give that employee a chance to indulge his or her personal passion at work.

▶ Idea

Brainstorm about the most logical areas for your library to aspire to "thought leadership." Content curation takes time and commitment. It makes most sense to focus your library's content curation on topics with which it is already familiar because this will reduce the learning curve for the staff providing the content, and it will also mean that the content curators can take advantage of the content that already exists at the library. However, at the same time, remember that one of the goals of content curation may be to increase awareness about your library with nonusers. To do this, you may decide that you need to become content experts in an area for which the library has no prior expertise. To help facilitate this process, make one list of topics about which it would be easy for the library to curate content because someone on the library staff is already an expert in that area. Examples include genealogy, writing, self-publishing, or poetry—all things that the library already understands. Then, make a second list of potential topics about which the library is not an expert but which might attract an audience of interest to the library. This list might include things like the local art scene or information about local landmarks or a summary of local politics or the newest consumer technologies. Consider the relative size of the audience for each topic and plan to allocate content curation resources accordingly. You do not want to become the expert in providing curated content around a topic that is so esoteric that it has an audience of only ten people. You do need to consider the potential return on the work that will go into content creation.

LEARNING

Once you have determined your audience and your topic of focus, content curation consists of finding, adding value, and sharing. Finding is the process of either creating or discovering the content that will have value for your audience of choice. There is more information in later sections of this chapter about some of the tools that are now available to make the process of finding content easier for the content curator. *Adding value* is making sense of the content. This is where the content curator inserts some element into the curation to enhance its value to the audience. These are some of the ways that a curator can add value:

- Identifying content that supports a theme (local oil painters in the community)
- Collecting content and providing commentary (ten local mystery writers with librarians' reviews of their most recent books)
- Doing the work to identify top-quality content (ten best websites to help you manage your money)
- Creating original content (a blog entry written by a librarian about the ten most important tools for Canadian genealogists)

Finally, *sharing* is putting together the content you have collected and providing it to your audience in an easy-to-read and easy-to-access format via social media, a blog, a website, and so forth.

▶ Idea

Review your library's website and social media channels to identify places where your library has already done content curation. In each case, consider how you have added value. Could you have done more to add value to the content? How might you have added value in a different, more effective way? Did library users respond to your content curation? An audit of what you have done to date will help you understand how you can adjust your curation to be more effective in the future. If you have simply grabbed content from websites and put it together in a list, the value is much less than if you have added commentary or edited content for only the best material.

LEARNING

Content curation is different from content aggregation. Content curation is about identifying quality information and adding value in some fashion to the content before it is shared with an audience. Content aggregation is an algorithmic process that identifies content of a similar nature with no effort to add value to the content via application of judgment, perspective, or research. Libraries aggregate information every day by providing lists of where to go for more information about topics. Sometimes those lists are curated to ensure that we are providing only quality research and sometimes they are not. There is little valued added to aggregations other than the fact that they are an easy way to identify multiple sources of information about the same topic. However, if the lists are curated, this means that someone has spent time and energy to review each resource, determine that it provides high-quality content that is true and reliable, and put it together with other content on the same topic. There is value in this because it allows the reader to go to one place to get a lot of reliable information—something we all need in our busy lives.

▶ Idea

See if you can find examples on your library's website of aggregated content versus curated content. What value does the curated content provide to you versus the aggregated content? Is there value in providing both to an audience?

LEARNING

Focus on providing quality *content.* The goal of content curation is to collect quality content and add value to it. The starting point is quality content, which is content that is reliable, well written, and has integrity, meaning that you know the original source and have read it. You are trying to make life easier for the person who looks at your curated content. You do not want to provide a pile of content that then has to be reviewed and sorted through before the reader can start using it. If that is what was wanted, the reader could do a Google search and start sorting without any help.

Adding value can mean many different things. It can simply be spending the time to find content that works together to illuminate a theme. It can be adding perspective to content that gives it an added dimension. It can be finding an unusual way of putting content together so that the reader suddenly has a completely different take on what he or she is reading. It can be writing original content. Bottom line: adding value means that the content curator puts time, thought, and energy into putting together content that will be useful to the audience for which that content is being created.

I read a good analogy for content curation referenced by Kevan Lee on the *BufferSocial* blog (https://blog.bufferapp.com/guide-to-content-curation) and provided originally by Mike Kaput on the Content Marketing Institute website (http://contentmarketinginsti tute.com/2014/04/what-medium-means-content-marketing). The gist was that for a long time, people seeking specific content online would go to the blogs and websites which provided that content only. We wanted milk, so we asked the milkman to deliver it. However, today, people are more interested in the Costco model. They want eggs and cereal and batteries, so they go to one spot to get it all. Content curation is the Costco model, saving time for others by digging up the good content and putting it all in one place.

▶ Idea

Develop a list of five to ten websites that provide content and plan to review them for two weeks. Identify why you chose each website. Accuracy, extensive knowledge about the topic, great writing, cutting-edge content—what is it about each website that makes it worth your time? Once you have created a list of what can be important with respect to curated content, prioritize the list. This will help guide you about what is important in curated content as you start curating.

LEARNING

Created, contributed, and collected content are the cornerstones of content curation. (For more on this idea, see Steve Rosenbaum's article "5 Tips for Great Content Curation" at http://mashable.com/2012/04/27/tips-great-content-curation.) As you start to collect content to curate, consider that it can come from any one of three sources. Content can be created, meaning that your library develops the original content. Content can be contributed, meaning that you invite visitors to your website to provide their own comments, ideas, and content. Finally, content can also be collected around specific topics or themes from information available on the Internet. A combination of all three types of information can be a strong format for content curation because it expands the reach of where you can go for content (not requiring you to create it all yourself) and it can create an interesting interaction of types of content. My suggestion is that if you are curating content about a specific topic, for every ten pieces of content, five are contributed, three are created, and two are collected to add variety to the topic (much like the 5-3-2 rule for social media content).

▶ Idea

Look around your library and identify already existing created, contributed, and collected content. Created content can be found in book reviews or movie guides written by librarians. It can be presentations done by authors that have been videotaped and shared online. It might be a how-to-do-it research video developed by a librarian. Contributed content might be a bit more difficult to find. Has your library ever asked the community to take over some aspect of its web services? For example, *Down East* magazine (the subject of chapter 8) asks the public once a month to take over its Instagram account for a weekend. That is contributed content. Another example would be if you asked your community to provide input about a library event or idea. Finally, collected content is probably what you will find the most, given that libraries have been doing this type of content curation for years. Librarians are experts at finding good-quality information and sharing that with library users so they can use the information. As you find different types of content, consider whether one type of information seems better than another or whether different types are appropriate for different scenarios.

LEARNING

Provide curated content across multiple channels, if possible. A channel is the method of content delivery. In broad terms, a channel can be any form of social media, like a website or blog, or it can be e-mail. The more channels your curated content touches, the more likely that you will reach the audience members with whom you want to build a relationship because they are most likely accessing multiple channels themselves. However, do not go down this path if you do not have the time and resources to keep up with content creation and management. You do not want to start attracting your audience using one channel only to discover that you just cannot find the time to keep managing that channel of delivery. You will lose the people who had already started following you and you will not get them back.

▶ Idea

As you start curating, experiment with different channels of delivery to see where you best get the attention of your chosen audience. Start with providing content via social media—Facebook, Pinterest, Instagram. Blogs are also great ways of providing curated content. You can also develop infographics, videos, podcasts, and slideshows. Ask for feedback from the people who access this content. Ask them what they like most and what is most useful to them.

LEARNING

Always credit the original creator of content. I think librarians know this one, so I do not have to spend a lot of time on it. I also think that content should always have a date attached to it to help the reader know how current it is. Information changes and is adapted so quickly today that if content is six months old around certain topics it could be completely outdated. I no longer use content if I cannot find a date attached to it because I am afraid of discovering some wonderful piece of information that will turn out to date back to 1984.

▶ Idea

Read the article "Content Curation: Copyright, Ethics and Fair Use" by Pawan Deshpande (www.contentcurationmarketing.com/content-curation-copyright-ethics-fair-use). This article provides a good overview of the dos and don'ts of content curation and will help you ensure that your library is using it in an ethical fashion.

LEARNING

There are a lot of places to go to collect content, so explore some of them to see what best meets your needs. You may go to one site for local community information and another if you are curating content that covers a broader area.

▶ Idea

Explore the following examples of the information collection tools that can help you in the process of content curation:

- Feedly.com will provide a whole set of websites and blogs, all focused on your search topic of interest.

- Alltop.com answers the question "What's happening?" in all of the topics of interest to you.
- BuzzFeed.com features feeds for breaking news, original reporting, entertainment, and video.
- ContentGems.com helps you find, curate, and share engaging content.

If you want to collect content at your local level, there are many different ways to do this. The following are some options:

- Set up a Google Alert (www.google.com/alerts) using search words that pertain to your community. For example, I have a Google Alert set to pop up every time Curtis Memorial Library comes up in the news.
- Use Twitter Search or Facebook Search to find local pages. You can then like and follow those pages to get a regular feed of information from your community.
- Use Topix.com to collect local information about your town.
- Read the local news resources.
- Collect content to curate on your own by going to local creators and asking for their participation.
- Search for "blogs" and "[your locale]."

LEARNING

Find content that interests and energizes you. Content curation is like anything else. If you get really excited about it and the topics around which you are going to focus, your energy and enthusiasm will come across clearly and the end result will be highly valuable content. If you are a librarian during the week and a singer on weekends, why not start curating a music-related Pinterest page at work that the library can use and you can have fun researching and creating? As long as the topics are focused on attracting the audience that your library wants, it only makes sense to give library employees an opportunity to build content based on what they love. One of the keys to ensuring quality content curation is to make sure that those who are involved in doing it are passionate about the topics.

▶ Idea

Ask one librarian to start curating content based on an area of special interest or aptitude that can be used to teach other library employees how to do the same. Give that person the freedom to curate content any way he or she wants about any topic of his or her choice. Use this content as a teaching tool for other library employees by demonstrating when content attracted a lot of attention, when there were problems getting attention, and so on.

LEARNING

Make unexpected connections for your audience members to help them see content in a new and different way. Do not forget that you can add value to content curation by making connections across content that other people might not have considered. This book is an example of doing just that. I went to a source of information (businesses) that libraries do not tend to think about as a source of information for ideas. I then translated what I learned into content in the form of ideas that libraries can use to experiment. You can try this yourself by going to normal sources of information and making unexpected connections. For example, trend spotters are people who look at the same newspapers, books, television shows, and movies that the rest of us see. However, they look for and spot connections among content that suggest that something is happening in more than one place, indicating that a trend is developing.

▶ Idea

Identify one service that you offer at your library and think about how you might curate content related to it. For example, if your library provides genealogy research, think about where you might go unexpectedly to curate content for genealogists. One example might be to collect content from the history of local jails. This might include the names of people who were inmates during a specific historical time period like the Civil War. You might include pictures from that period and newspaper articles about the jail from the local paper. Your content is valuable to genealogists because you are providing access to a collection of information about ancestors that a genealogy researcher might never have considered.

LEARNING

Consider curating an online magazine. This might not work for every library out there. But if you have the resources, why not consider developing an online magazine focused on a specific topic? This type of content curation sounds difficult, but with today's available software and technology, it is actually relatively easy to do. Here are a couple of tools that can help you publish the content that you curate in an attractive magazine format:

- Scoop.it helps you collect content in a magazine format that you can then publish on your website or blog if you want.
- CLIPZINE helps you collect images and then create magazines based on those images that you can also publish to your website or blog.

If you are interested in learning more about the different types of content curation tools available, check out Meg Sutton's "Content Curation Tools: The Ultimate List" (www.curata.com/blog/content-curation-tools-the-ultimate-list).

▶ Idea

Try out one of the digital magazine tools to see if it will work for your library. These tools are fun to try out and the end result is very professional looking. Think about the audience that you want to attract with content curation and whether a clean magazine look might be helpful in attracting that audience.

LEARNING

Do not forget to market your content curation to ensure that your target audience is aware of the valuable information that you are providing. Content curation works only if the audience that you want to attract finds the content and looks at it. Once you get people used to using the content, they will look for new content on their own. However, you have to make sure that they make that original connection. So, if you plan to do content curation, you also need to think about how you will do initial marketing to make sure that your desired audience knows you are providing content and makes that initial contact. You do not have to do a long-term marketing program. Rather, your goal is simply to develop awareness in your targeted audience that the library is providing fantastic content around a topic of interest and direct the audience to that content. After that, it will be up to the individuals to decide if they like that content and want more of it.

▶ Idea

After you have identified two to three audiences that your library would like to attract with content curation, think about how you will reach those audiences to inform them about the library's content curation. If an audience is part of the already existing library user base, then there are lots of ways to develop initial awareness. It will be harder if you are trying to reach an audience that does not normally use the library. Think about how these audiences move through your community. Is there someplace that you know they "touch" every day where you might put materials about the content curation? For example, if you want to reach young parents, consider leaving information with day care providers. Is there another organization in the community that works with this audience that might help you get the word out? For example, if you would like to attract new local artists, is there an Arts Alliance that might be willing to help share information about the library's content curation? When you market, remember to make the information as short and simple as possible: What are you raising awareness about? Where can it be found? Is there a cost associated with accessing it? Who is providing it? Your goal is only to get people to take the action step of finding the content curation and checking it out. After that, the content has to sell itself.

• THE BIG IDEAS FROM THE RESEARCH •

The whole concept of content curation is a big idea for me. I know how libraries curate content, but I had never thought about it in the context of using content curation as a way of attracting new audiences for a library. The biggest issue with it for libraries is the perceived amount of time and resources involved in providing curated content. My response to that is that there are many tools now available to help facilitate the process of collecting and curating content. In addition, it makes sense to keep the number of topics for content curation small while you experiment and try out different options. Content curation is such a potentially powerful tool to use in attracting new library users, and because it builds on the skills and experience in curating content that librarians already have, it just begs to be tried!

If you are interested in seeing an example of content curation that is being done at Curtis Memorial Library, check out our Curtis Creative Spaces website (http://curtiscreativespaces.com). The goals of the website are to (a) increase awareness among local creators (artists, musicians, writers) about the library's resources and (b) increase awareness among library users about the work of local creators. Our value-added element in this curation is providing access to local creators. This is still a work in progress, but hopefully it will build over time.

• SUMMARY OF WHAT I LEARNED •

- Content curation is useful to libraries because it can help them build relationships with new audiences in their communities.
- Before you start curating content, identify the audience that you want to reach and why you want to reach that audience.
- Identify the topics for content curation about which your library can become a sought-out source of information in the community.

- Once you have determined your audience and your topic of focus, content curation consists of finding, adding value, and sharing.
- Content curation is different from content aggregation.
- Focus on creating *quality* content.
- Created, contributed, and collected content are the cornerstones of content curation.
- Provide curated content across multiple channels, if possible.
- Always credit the original creator of content.
- There are a lot of places to go to collect content, so explore some of them to see what best meets your needs.
- Find content that interests and energizes you.
- Make unexpected connections for your audience members to help them see content in a new and different way.
- Consider curating an online magazine.
- Do not forget to market your content curation to ensure that your target audience is aware of the valuable information that you are providing.

• RESOURCES •

"The Busy Person's Guide to Content Curation: A 3-Step Process for Your Blog, Newsletter, or Timeline," by Kevan Lee, *BuffSocial* (blog), May 5, 2014, http://blog.bufferapp.com/guide-to-content-curation

"Content Curation: Copyright, Ethics and Fair Use," by Pawan Deshpande, Content Curation Marketing, February 20, 2013, www.contentcurationmarketing.com/content-curation-copyright-ethics-fair-use

"Content Curation Primer," by Beth Kanter, *Beth's Blog*, October 4, 2011, www.bethkanter.org/content-curation-101

"Content Curation Tools: The Ultimate List," by Meg Sutton, *Content Marketing Forum* (blog), March 28, 2014, www.curata.com/blog/content-curation-tools-the-ultimate-list

11

UNCONVENTIONAL THINKING

KATE CHENEY CHAPPELL
Tom's of Maine

• WHY THIS TOPIC •

I think that the most effective future library leaders will be individuals who have a broad experience base, having worked in many different types of jobs. They will know how to meld the disparity of what they have learned into an unconventional, nontraditional, and very powerful set of skills. The library profession will seek out and embrace people who bring experience in law or business or entrepreneurship or any other profession (in addition to librarianship) to their role as library directors, seeing the value and vitality that the breadth of this experience will bring to the leadership of a public library. These individuals will be able to run their libraries as skillfully as any library director in the past, but they will also bring new innovation and imagination to that process, derived from the integration of learning from the different parts of their lives. They will be open to learning from others, they will be unconventional in how they apply that learning, and they will be willing to use good ideas, regardless of where the ideas originated. My goal for this entire book was to learn from unconventional thinkers, so I think it makes sense to end the book with a chapter that explores this topic.

• WHY THIS ORGANIZATION •

Tom's of Maine has always intrigued me because it is a company that was developed and run in a very unique way. The founders (Tom and Kate Cheney Chappell) built a corporate enterprise that was centered on respecting the environment and delivering high-quality, natural consumer oral care products that people wanted to buy. They figured out how to integrate the two ideas successfully, and they did it on their own terms, building a company rooted in values. Having worked in the corporate world myself for many years, I admire the courage and creativity involved in doing this and think that they are a great example of leaders who are willing to embrace and use what they have learned in new and progressive ways.

Kate Cheney Chappell kindly agreed to an interview with me after she did a talk at Curtis Memorial Library about her work as an artist. During her talk, she mentioned a tool that she uses at Tom's of Maine called a "connecting exercise." Essentially, a connecting exercise is a process in which a group reads a chosen poem and after a brief discussion pairs up to share life experiences based on questions arising from the poem. The goal is to use poetry to help people open up to their own and others' thoughts. I love the idea of using poetry to get people to think along new paths in a business environment because it is so unconventional. This is exactly the type of creativity and willingness to use nontraditional ideas that I think libraries need to learn, so I asked Kate if I could interview her.

As I talked with Kate, it became clear that she has learned to use her skills wherever they would be useful, regardless of whether doing so is traditional or the norm. She employs her sensibilities as an artist in her work as an entrepreneur at Tom's of Maine. In the art world, she utilizes her entrepreneurial skills to develop collaborations with other artists, resulting in initiatives such as the Envelope Project, an artist's book of envelopes that she made with twenty-one other women based on Maxine Kumin's poem "The Envelope," containing the words and images of daughters about their mothers. Kate has figured out how to integrate very different skills so that she uses them all in her life versus employing one or the other. She has determined how to be her own person, holding true to her values and looking at the world with the eye of an artist even while she operates as a businessperson. I wanted to explore how she has done this in the hopes of identifying new ways for the library profession to do the same. We spent an afternoon together talking about both Tom's of Maine and Kate's perspective as an artist.

• INSIGHTS FROM THIS INTERVIEW •

LEARNING

If you want a culture that is comfortable with the unconventional, with experimentation and ambiguity, the people running the organization must have a clearly defined vision of where they are going and they need to model the behavior that they think will get the organization to that end point. Developing a new type of organization can be daunting. People question why you are doing what you are doing and frequently challenge new ways of working. I asked Kate how the leadership at Tom's of Maine developed a culture that was comfortable with doing things so differently from the business norms of the time. Tom's had innovative product development practices, personnel policies (offering maternity and paternity leave prior to the Family and Medical Leave Act), and communications with the consumer (including the first full ingredient disclosure prior to the mandate for this) long before any of those things were standard business practices. Tom's was also an innovator in community commitment. The company initiated a 10 percent charitable giving commitment when the norm for corporate contributions was in the range of 2 percent of pretax earnings. Going beyond this financial commitment, the company instituted a policy of giving employees 5 percent paid time off to help the nonprofit of their choice in their community. These practices are still in place today. In addition, Kate brought poetry into the Tom's of Maine boardroom through her use of the connecting exercises, and she used art to help develop teamwork among all of the employees at the company. Tom's definitely did not conform to the business norms of the times (the early 1970s).

Kate's response was that she and Tom were both very comfortable modeling the behavior they wanted to see at Tom's and believed strongly that the path they were taking was the right one. They had a clear vision of where they wanted Tom's to go, and they were both very good communicators who could share their vision with power and passion. Working inclusively and collaboratively with all of the Tom's of Maine employees and the company's board, Tom and Kate developed the Tom's of Maine statement of beliefs (the values that guide the company) and mission statement (the goals of the company based on those values). Beyond that, they made "living the mission" an ongoing process by cycling new employees through the training curriculum that they developed, titled the "Seven Intentions of Values-Centered Leadership." The clay exercise that you will read about further on in this chapter was developed by Kate as part of the "Venture Out" Intention. Finally, Kate and Tom were not afraid to integrate their experiences from other parts of their lives into their work as entrepreneurs, and they were perfectly comfortable asking others to experiment and do the same.

▶ Implication

Library leaders must have a clear vision for the library's future, be able to articulate that vision and how the library will achieve it in a compelling way, model the behaviors that will make it happen, and be open to unconventional ways of working to achieve their vision. Being able to articulate a clear vision about where your library is going can be an intimidating concept to library directors. We are practical people who spend a great deal of our time in the day-to-day running of our organizations. It seems somehow a bit overreaching to talk about the "vision" for the library. But if you do not have a clear sense of where the organization is supposed to go, why should anyone be willing to follow you? In the article "What Leading with Vision Really Means" (www.fastcompany.com/3003293/what-leading-vision-really-means), Erika Andersen states that you need to have your organization's goal clearly defined so that when problems arise people know that there is value in working through the issues to the end point. They also need to know that a leader is committed to the vision because it is the right thing to do, not because it is self-serving for that individual. People want to feel like they are part of something that matters and that is bigger than the individuals involved. When they feel this way, commitment to the vision follows.

What does it look like to live the behavior that you want to see? You clearly define your expectations. You talk every day about the values that you want to see displayed in your organization and your message is consistent. You do what you say. If you want an open culture in which people address issues directly with one another, then you act that way when you are involved in conflict. If you want your library's customer service to be outstanding, then you discuss customer service daily, provide employees with training about customer service, and address problems with customer service immediately. You give employees clear direction in their job descriptions about the library's expectations with respect to its values. When employees exhibit the desired values, you reward them.

Finally, library leaders need to be open to unconventional ways of working for one reason. We cannot keep doing what we have always done and expect that this will provide us with the level of creativity and innovation that we need to move the library forward as a flourishing community institution. Openness to what is new, along with the desire to integrate learning from all aspects of our lives into our profession as librarians, is what will produce the public library director for the next century.

▶ Idea

Develop a list of the behaviors that you think should be exhibited in your library based on what you have conveyed to your employees as the library's leader. Evaluate your own performance in modeling those behaviors. You can do this by simply reading through the list and giving yourself an A, B, C, or D grade or rating yourself on a scale. However you do it, when you are done, ask another library employee (or several) to go through the list and rate you on the same factors. Compare your scores to those of the other individuals evaluating you. If there are areas of major discrepancy, consider whether these are areas where you need to do a better job of "walking the walk" for your library.

Talk with the folks who did the ranking and consider their input. What can you learn from their comments? What can you do with more consistency to model the behaviors that should be important at your library? Identify one to three things that you can start doing differently to do a better job of modeling.

LEARNING

Giving people tools that help them connect (with one another or with their own thoughts/feelings/values) can take down barriers and improve the work that they are trying to do. Kate and I talked a great deal about the connecting exercises that she has used throughout her career as an entrepreneur, artist, and poet. I was interested in the concept because it seemed to be such a unique way to build bridges between people and to help individuals connect to themselves. Kate kindly gave me permission to share examples of how she has used the exercise in the past; one such example appears at the end of this chapter after the interview questions (see *Connecting* exercise, page 221).

Briefly, here is how you conduct the exercise. Share a poem with a group. The poem should have some relationship to the work being done by the group, and it needs to be short enough to be read slowly. Then, ask several directed questions of the group to help them consider the poem and what thoughts and feelings it raises in them. After a few minutes of thinking, have people pair up to share life experiences based on questions arising from the poem.

The goal of this process is to give people a way to connect with one another and/or with their own thoughts via the use of poetry. Poetry, because of its brevity, can be an extraordinarily powerful way of opening up thoughts and feelings that the reader did not even know were there. By sharing thoughts and feelings with another person, this exercise can be a wonderful way to break down barriers between people and open them up to connect with their own core thoughts, values, and wisdom. In turn, this can help them think in new ways about problems or to find new paths forward around specific issues. Once the connecting exercise is completed, the group then goes on to consider the issues at hand, hopefully with clearer heads and more open, receptive thought processes.

▶ Implication

Try a connecting exercise when your library encounters a roadblock or problem.
I am a fan of the connecting exercise as developed and used by Kate.
I like organizational tools that are nonlinear and unusual because
they tend to nudge people's thoughts in new directions. I also think
this process could be very powerful with librarians. We are already
primed to love and respond to literature. Why not use that innate
tendency for the benefit of the library?

▶ Idea

*Ask a librarian who is a poetry lover to develop a connecting exercise focused on
a specific issue or opportunity that your library is facing.* This person needs
to identify a relevant poem and several questions that will help the
readers think about the poem and connect with their own thoughts
or values. After some time reading and thinking about the poem,
people can pair up to discuss their insights. Once the connecting
exercise is completed, the group should then move on to address
the issue at hand. Afterward, ask the librarian about the impact of
the connecting exercise. Did he or she think that the exercise was
helpful in getting the group to be more thoughtful and open to others? Ask this librarian to share the concept with other librarians who
are interested in it. Keep trying this exercise in different scenarios
until you identify where and how it works best in your library.

LEARNING

*There is value in learning to see the reality of what is in front of you versus the
symbol of what is in front of you.* Kate and I discussed how artists develop
their own eye, or way of looking at the world. Everyone has a vision
in his or her mind of what a tree looks like (it has branches, a trunk,
roots, leaves). This is what artists call a symbol of a tree. It is a symbol
because it is a universally understood image of a tree. It is a sign
pointing to the here-and-now tree being witnessed, but it is not the
actual tree. An artist is trained to look at a tree and focus on seeing
much more than the symbol of a tree. An artist looks at colors,
shades, planes, contours, and positive and negative space. By doing

this, the artist sees more of the *reality* of the tree as compared to the symbol of the tree. The assumption is that the image developed in this way is much richer than the symbol of the object because it has so much more information about the object and is therefore closer to the reality of it.

▶ Implication

If libraries can learn to look at their communities with an eye that goes beyond surface details, they can develop an image of what their communities need and want that will be so much richer and full of information than what they have today. Libraries have been in existence for a very long time. Library employees have learned to see their communities a certain way. We think we know what our library users want and need because we assume that we have a clear vision of who those people are. What if our vision is something that was developed twenty or thirty years ago and is no longer valid? What if we have a vision based on five to ten people who are in the library regularly but who, in fact, are not representational of the community at all?

By making a concentrated effort to look closely at our communities of service and see them with a new eye, we can increase our understanding of their richness and depth. There are so many ways to do this. Library employees can volunteer to participate on community committees. A library could execute a community survey, asking both library users and nonusers about their perceptions of the library. A library could ask for community volunteers to participate in focus groups to discuss what is happening in their lives with which the library might be able to help by providing programs, services, or information. The more libraries can do to clarify and deepen how they see the communities that they serve, the better able they will be to provide appropriate services and products for those communities.

I think this same point holds true with library patrons, many of whom have been going to the library for years and years. We see them and think we know them. It cannot hurt us as librarians to try to look a second time at even our oldest, most loyal patrons to make sure we are really seeing them. Do we know if their interests in reading have changed? Do they understand all of the new services being offered at the library? Is there an opportunity for the library to do more to help them with their lives? Think about teens in your library or the homeless people who use your library. Do you look at an individual and immediately see "teen" or "homeless person"? If so, you are looking at the symbol of a person instead of trying to see the real person.

▶ Idea

Working with a team of library employees, develop a statement that defines the community that your library serves. Use that statement as the starting point for a discussion with your library leadership. What do they think is right, what is wrong, and what is missing in that statement? Where else would they recommend that you go to get a more complete understanding of the community? Get feedback, make adjustments, and then ask a group of community members to spend an hour at the library providing their feedback. Again, where would they recommend that you go to get a broader perspective? Continue to ask different groups for their feedback and adjust your statement accordingly. You are not seeking a final, complete statement in this exercise. Rather, you are working to develop an ongoing process of discovery about your community that will help you learn more about it.

LEARNING

As an artist, you learn to stop seeing in a habitual way in order to truly see. Kate talked about using an exercise that she developed to teach people at Tom's to see differently in order to think creatively about new products. New product development was Kate's responsibility at Tom's, and innovative thinking is the first step. The goal of the exercise as used at Tom's is to teach trust in self, how to work with others, and how to see differently. Here is Kate's description:

> A group of four people sit at a table, each with a mound of clay on a paper plate. They agree to be blindfolded, then are asked to make something with clay, whatever

their hands want. The emphasis is on letting the hands do the work. No one can see, so that helps give confidence to try. After fifteen minutes, blindfolds come off and people look at what they have made. They are often surprised that it resembles what they had in mind. Objects are shared, then all clay is put to the center, and without blindfolds, the "team" of four is asked to come up with a "new product"—something original. After a half hour of working together, they present these team creations to the whole group. Over the years, I have witnessed some amazing "inventions" and, more importantly, seen people go from thinking "I can't do that" to trusting their own innate creativity (in the first exercise) and in the team approach (in the second). [All rights reserved, Kate Cheney Chappell]

▶ Implication

If libraries want to develop new operational models for the future, they need to look for new sources of ideas and inspiration. If libraries have to evolve to stay relevant in their communities, then it makes sense that they find new processes and tools that will help them get there. If librarians keep doing things the way we always have (habitual action), we need to expect that we will find incremental versus transformational improvements. The alternative (which sounds like a lot more fun to me) is to throw caution to the wind, try new ideas and ways of seeing, and not stop until we hit that breakthrough moment that proves that we can trust our own innate creativity.

▶ Idea

Get a copy of Drawing on the Right Side of the Brain: A Course in Enhancing Creativity and Artistic Confidence, *by Betty Edwards (Penguin, 2012), and try one of the exercises with your staff.* Kate suggested trying "Upside Down Drawing" and "Vases and Faces" as being exercises that would be particularly helpful for groups of librarians. At the end of the meeting, ask if the exercise had any impact on their thinking in the meeting. Were they more open to new ideas? Did they feel like they were any more creative? The goal of going through exercises like these is to demonstrate how helpful it can be to go to a nontraditional place in your mind to help you see things in a new way. Plus, as Kate said to me, it is a great way of improving your drawing skills.

LEARNING

Entrepreneurs look at their environment and say, "Sure, we can do that!" and trust that they can use their ability to think creatively to figure out answers. When people are unconventional thinkers, they are comfortable with their ability to learn new things and move in new directions. Kate talked about the Tom's of Maine product line in the early years of the company. It was comprised of products in three different sectors: an agricultural product that was a dairy cleaner with no phosphates; a product called LiftOff that would clean up oil spills and was sold to oil dealers making deliveries; and a consumer detergent that also did not contain phosphates. As they developed the company, it became clear that the opportunity for Tom's was to develop direct-to-the-consumer products like soap, toothpaste, and shampoo. So, ultimately, they let go of the industrial products and focused on the consumer side, and Tom's of Maine became a personal care company delivering natural oral care products. Bottom line: they identified an opportunity, figured out how to make that opportunity work for them, and then took the leap of faith to make it happen. They did not say to themselves, "We create industrial products; we can't make consumer products." Rather, they asked themselves, "How do we make this happen?"

▶ Implication

Libraries will stay relevant and useful if they are able to be nimble, responsive to their environment, and open to new ideas. I think this idea has very broad and important implications for libraries. We will be relevant to our communities only if we are useful. We will be able to be useful only if we are able to identify, understand, and respond *quickly* to the needs of our communities, and this requires that we be nimble. The world in which we live simply moves too quickly for us to be able to ponder, think about, and test ideas for months at a time, only to come out with a product that is free but hard to access or complicated to understand or difficult to use. The expectations of library users are set in the consumer marketplace, and for better or worse, those are the standards to which libraries will be held. Librarians need to become comfortable with making mistakes, moving quickly, taking risks, and sometimes not succeeding.

As important, we need to make sure that we set appropriate expectations with our funding authorities about the new world in which libraries operate. We need to teach our funders that libraries are becoming much more entrepreneurial in how they operate and much less like a lumbering municipal department. We will test new ideas and programs with the goal of better meeting the needs of our communities. Sometimes we will be wildly successful and sometimes we will fail. However, failure is essential to helping us move forward in new ways. A key message that we need to convey through all of this is that libraries, again mirroring entrepreneurial organizations, will be exceptionally careful with their funding in this process. They will not commit to spending a lot of money until they have tested an idea and know it will work. They will be responsible with the support provided. The end result will be a win-win for the communities that libraries serve—better services provided in as efficient a method as possible.

Libraries will not be willing to step out on a ledge and try new ideas if they think that they will lose all credibility with the people who pay the bills. How do librarians make sure this does not happen? I think it goes back to a clear articulation of the vision and values for the library that gets shared throughout the community. You back that up with library leaders who model what they are saying. Finally, you do research with the library's community to understand how community members are responding and be flexible enough to adjust as necessary based on the community's input.

▶ Ideas

Start to talk in your library about what it means to be nimble. This might take the form of having brown-bag lunches for staff and volunteers at which there is a general discussion about what it means to move quickly and to be responsive to the community that the library serves. Another idea would be to develop a wall somewhere in the library where staff can post examples of nimble behavior, either in your library or another library, and where comments can be written next to the behavior. The goal is to start having everyone on the library's staff begin thinking and talking about the idea of being quick to learn from and respond to the environment. Once people start being aware of nimbleness as a concept, ask them to apply it to the work they are doing in the library. How can they speed up their responses? What can you as a library leader do to facilitate fast actions on the part of the library? What can the library leadership do to support this concept?

Start talking with the funding authority for your library about what it means to have a nimble, entrepreneurial library. This is not a one-time conversation. You need to explain why libraries must change and the risks and rewards involved in changing. You need to share your strategic mission, vision, and values and answer questions about why these strategic documents are so important. Your goal is to get your library's funders to understand what your library is trying to do and its impact on your community. In addition, this conversation will help the library's leaders identify concepts that are problematic for the library's funders. This is important because you want to make sure you address those concerns as quickly as possible.

LEARNING

There is no established path to help you find truly new ways of working. The last part of my discussion with Kate was about the artist's desire to find a method of working that is right for him or her and that comes from a place of originality. Artists often look at the work of other artists out of general interest. However, every artist wants to develop his or her own original work that is like no one else's. This process is frequently a struggle, as artists try to find a new way of creating the art that speaks to them. As Kate said, "I feel like I'm doing original work when I don't know what I'm doing. You don't have a map." Kate did not seem be particularly uncomfortable about not having a map. To unconventional thinkers, working without a map is just how you do business.

▶ Implication

There is no one right way for libraries to evolve, so their best tools are a willingness to grab good ideas, regardless of their origin, and to strive to think differently. This is a great thought on which to end this book. As I interviewed people, I learned a tremendous amount. I found new ideas for doing a better job leading my library. I discovered ways of working that could be truly transformational. However, what also became clear is that there is no one right way to move forward. The key is to be willing to search for new ideas and processes in every place that seems like it might be a good resource and then to move forward, not always knowing what you are doing. Be willing to take risks, make mistakes, and learn from those mistakes. You will figure it out, and your community will benefit from having a library that is a living, evolving entity.

• THE BIG IDEAS FROM THIS INTERVIEW •

The learning "If you want a culture that is comfortable with the unconventional, with experimentation and ambiguity, the people running the organization must have a clearly defined vision of where they are going and they need to model the behavior that they think will get the organization to that end point" is so important. Based on my own experience, I think there is opportunity for library leaders to do all of these things more often and with greater passion. Libraries are going through such periods of change that the more librarians can do to articulate the value of the change (instead of bemoaning it as the end of everything) and show by example how to move through that change, the better off our institutions will be and the more likely that change will be positive.

Finally, I learned from the entire interview with Kate that people who are creative, unconventional thinkers do not think in silos. They integrate what they have learned both professionally and personally. They are able to make transformative leaps in thinking because they are willing to make unexpected connections between things that do not normally relate to each other (like using poetry in business). They are constantly scanning their environment for good ideas, and they use them all. There is so much power and potential in this idea for libraries if library leaders can start thinking this way.

• SUMMARY OF WHAT I LEARNED •

- If you want a culture that is comfortable with the unconventional, with experimentation and ambiguity, the people running the organization must have a clearly defined vision of where they are going and they need to model the behavior that they think will get the organization to that end point.
- Giving people tools that help them connect (with one another or with their own thoughts/feelings/values) can take down barriers and improve the work that they are trying to do.
- There is value in learning to see the reality of what is in front of you versus the symbol of what is in front of you.
- As an artist, you learn to stop seeing in a habitual way in order to truly see.
- Entrepreneurs look at their environment and say, "Sure, we can do that!" and trust that they can use their ability to think creatively to figure out answers.
- There is no established path to help you find truly new ways of working.

• RESOURCES •

Drawing on the Right Side of the Brain: A Course in Enhancing Creativity and Artistic Confidence, by Betty Edwards (Penguin, 2012)

Kate Cheney Chappell Art Space, http://katechappellartspace
.com

*Managing Upside Down: The Seven Intentions of Values-Centered
Leadership,* by Tom Chappell (William Morrow, 1999)

The Natural Way to Draw: A Working Plan for Art Study, by
Kimon Nicolaïdes (Houghton Mifflin, 2010)

"What Leading with Vision Really Means," by Erika Andersen,
Fast Company, November 21, 2012, www.fastcompany
.com/3003293/what-leading-vision-really-means

• INTERVIEW QUESTIONS •

I read the materials on your website about being an artist,
and the thing that spoke to me as a librarian in particular
was: "my growing conviction that art could be the
connective tissue of a society, a force for building and
sustaining relationships" and "the relational aspect of art."
I certainly feel that way about art, but I also thought that
you could say the same about libraries—that they are one
of the many connective tissues of a community. Do you see
any of the same role for the public library? If yes, how? If
no, why not?

Do you have any thoughts about how to move an institution
that was/is centered around a thing (the book) into an
organization centered around values (building or
connecting community)?

How did you and Tom develop a new paradigm in your own
heads of what a business should be? Or did you start with
your product idea and back into the business model?

How did you build an organization that supported that
model?

Did you ever run into resistance? How did you deal with that?

How did you create a culture permeated with your values?

Do you think there is anything in particular that an
organization can do that will keep it from evolving and
changing? How would you address those issues?

You and Tom obviously had tremendous passion for the products that you developed at Tom's of Maine. How did you maintain that passion through all of the ups and downs of building your own business?

I read a quote by the artist Alfredo Jaar (a conceptual artist who explores unequal power relationships): "I strongly believe that artists are thinkers, as opposed to object makers. My working process is 99 percent thinking, and 1 percent making. That thinking process is at the core of what I do." If you ran an organization that was weighted heavily the other way (more doing than thinking), what might you do to get people to stop and think as a new way of operating?

Artists see life in a different way. They look at the world around them and see things that other people might never notice. How do you (or can you) open that eye in the average person so that they start looking at their work environment and the community that they serve differently?

"Failing up" or resiliency is supposed to be another trait of creative individuals. How do you think people learn to do this?

CONNECTING EXERCISE*

Shareholder's Annual Meeting
Tom's of Maine Community Center
Kennebunk, Maine
November 10, 2004—2:00 PM

Over the years I have found that reading a poem is a great way to get a meeting started. Instead of jumping right on the agenda, poetry gives us a chance to know each other better at a heart level. You can get to a very deep level quickly.

* ALL RIGHTS RESERVED BY KATE CHENEY CHAPPELL

Today I have chosen a poem by one of my favorite poets, Denise Levertov—her writing spanned over fifty years in the last half of the twentieth century—because of the economy of the words, the balance, the rhythm . . .

I do this at every board meeting and at many company-wide meetings. I love reading poetry (as well as writing it), so I always have a rich store to choose from.

The *Jacob's Ladder* collection, which I am proud was signed by her, contains the poem I am going to read, "The Fountain," and is one of her early ones. It seems a good time to read a poem that has hope at its core, hope linked to the idea of water. Our Rivers Program and Common Good Partnerships have done a lot to heighten awareness of this essential, precious resource. Let's listen to Levertov's poem and see how she uses water as a metaphor.

The Fountain

Don't say, don't say there is no water
to solace the dryness at our hearts.
I have seen

the fountain springing out of the rock wall
and you drinking there. And I too
before your eyes

found footholds and climbed
to drink the cool water.

The woman of that place, shading her eyes,
frowned as she watched—but not because
she grudged the water,

only because she was waiting
to see we drank our fill and were
refreshed.

Don't say, don't say there is no water.
That fountain is there among its scalloped
green and gray stones,

it is still there and always there
with its quiet song and strange power
to spring in us,

up and out through the rock.

• GENERAL DISCUSSION QUESTIONS •

1. What is the water symbolizing in this poem? What can satisfy our emotional thirst, "solace the dryness at our hearts"?
2. What is the importance of seeing others drink from "the fountain springing out of the rock wall"?
3. Who is the woman—what does she represent for you?
4. She repeats the line "Don't say, don't say there is no water." Who in our world is telling us there is no water?
5. There is a strong affirmation in the last stanza that "it [the fountain] is still there and always there / with its quiet song and strange power / to spring in us"—what does the poet mean by this and how are we like the rock through which the water springs up and out?

Pair up. Share your reflections with each other in answer to this question. Are you in a dry place in your heart? Do you feel that the fountain is there—ready to spring? Or is your heart overflowing?

INDEX

H
"hackathon," 48
hierarchy, 68, 69–71
hiring
    for organizational fit/attitude,
        178–180
    process at Gelato Fiasco, 20
    process unique to needs of organiza-
        tion, 22–25
"How to Be Creative" (Lehrer), 57
"How to Build Your Creative Confi-
    dence" (Kelley), 75
Hulu, 132–133
human needs, 124–126, 128

I
idea central, 65–66
ideal person statement, 179–180
ideas
    brainstorming ideas from what you
        learned, 6
    brilliance, not setting out for, 62–63
    consumer trends, identification of,
        126–129
    in creative environment, 42–43
    creativity from lack of ego, 67–68
    developing/examining ideas for
        sense of sight, 60–62
    e-mail inbox for, 13
    employee ideas, tracking sheet for, 171
    fermentation of, 6, 53–54
    from individual thinking, 47–49
    for library service, 72
    narrowing focus of, 6–7
    new sources of inspiration, looking
        for, 214–215
    new ways of working, no established
        path for, 218
    nurturing in safe environment,
        68–69
    positive reinforcement for flow of,
        64–66
    problem-solving pool for library,
        43–44
    storytelling for interest in, 83–86
    testing by libraries, 13–14
    in trend tracking, 130
    from trend tracking, RFPC for,
        138–139
ideas, big
    from advocates for the creators inter-
        view, 94–95

from content curation research, 202
from creativity interview, 55–56
from customer service interview,
    118–119
from entrepreneurship interview, 32
from learning your community inter-
    view, 157–158
from seeing extraordinary in the
    ordinary interview, 74
from trend tracking interview, 139
from unconventional thinking inter-
    view, 218–219
from workplace interview, 180–181
"I'm not creative" assumption, 54–55
improvement, 66–67
individual thinking, 47–49
information
    collection of information about your
        beat, daily, 155–156
    consumer trends, identification
        of for understanding change,
        126–129
    means for people to get information
        to you, 152–153
    trust in workplace, communication
        for, 176–177
*Inside the Box: A Proven System of Creativ-
    ity for Breakthrough Results* (Boyd &
    Goldenberg), 53
Internet, 131–133
    See also technology; website
interview
    benefits of outside interactions, 1–2
    by Gelato Fiasco, 20, 22–23
    for hiring process, 23–25
    key steps in the process, 2–7
    by Maine Community Foundation,
        178–179
    process for, development of, 2
interview questions
    advocates for the creators, 96–97
    creativity, 57–58
    customer service, 120–122
    entrepreneurship, 33–35
    learning your community, 159–160
    for seeing extraordinary in the
        ordinary, 76
    trend tracking, 141–142
    unconventional thinking, 220–221
    workplace, 182–183
interviewee
    interview with, tips for, 5